TypeScript 3.0 Quick Guide

The easiest way to learn TypeScript

Patrick Desjardins

BIRMINGHAM - MUMBAI

TypeScript 3.0 Quick Start Guide

Copyright © 2018 Packt Publishing

All rights reserved. No part of this book may be reproduced, stored in a retrieval system, or transmitted in any form or by any means, without the prior written permission of the publisher, except in the case of brief quotations embedded in critical articles or reviews.

Every effort has been made in the preparation of this book to ensure the accuracy of the information presented. However, the information contained in this book is sold without warranty, either express or implied. Neither the author, nor Packt Publishing or its dealers and distributors, will be held liable for any damages caused or alleged to have been caused directly or indirectly by this book.

Packt Publishing has endeavored to provide trademark information about all of the companies and products mentioned in this book by the appropriate use of capitals. However, Packt Publishing cannot guarantee the accuracy of this information.

Commissioning Editor: Richa Tripathi
Acquisition Editor: Noyonika Das
Content Development Editor: Kirk Dsouza
Technical Editor: Shweta Jadhav
Copy Editor: Safis Editing
Project Coordinator: Hardik Bhinde
Proofreader: Safis Editing
Indexer: Aishwarya Gangawane
Graphics: Jason Monteiro
Production Coordinator: Shraddha Falebhai

First published: August 2018

Production reference: 1280818

Published by Packt Publishing Ltd.
Livery Place
35 Livery Street
Birmingham
B3 2PB, UK.

ISBN 978-1-78934-557-5

www.packtpub.com

mapt.io

Mapt is an online digital library that gives you full access to over 5,000 books and videos, as well as industry leading tools to help you plan your personal development and advance your career. For more information, please visit our website.

Why subscribe?

- Spend less time learning and more time coding with practical eBooks and Videos from over 4,000 industry professionals

- Improve your learning with Skill Plans built especially for you

- Get a free eBook or video every month

- Mapt is fully searchable

- Copy and paste, print, and bookmark content

PacktPub.com

Did you know that Packt offers eBook versions of every book published, with PDF and ePub files available? You can upgrade to the eBook version at www.PacktPub.com and as a print book customer, you are entitled to a discount on the eBook copy. Get in touch with us at service@packtpub.com for more details.

At www.PacktPub.com, you can also read a collection of free technical articles, sign up for a range of free newsletters, and receive exclusive discounts and offers on Packt books and eBooks.

Contributors

About the author

Patrick Desjardins has been working as a senior software developer for Netflix since 2017 and also is a senior software developer at Microsoft, working on MSDN, VSTS, and Teams. He was Microsoft's Most Valuable Professional (MVP) in ASP.NET for the years of 2013 and 2014. His area of interest is web development, which he has embraced since the early 2000s.

Patrick is a huge fan of Microsoft technologies, such as .NET, which he has developed with professionally since 2004. By contrast, in 2002 he started to develop many projects in PHP, which provides him multiple perspectives on how the web can be developed.

Patrick owns many open source projects and has written several books recently.

> *I dedicate this book to my wife, Melodie Savaria, who has been patient during the time I took to write this book and all the other projects I am incubating. I also dedicate this work to my parents, who opened the path to all my realizations, present and future. Finally, I dedicate this book to my daughter, Alicia, who I hope will never give up and always stretch beyond her dreams.*

About the reviewer

Alejandro Lora Gomez is a software developer residing in Seville, Spain. He is an instructor at Udemy, where he teaches his best-selling courses on Android and Kotlin to over 30,000 students. Alejandro has a keen interest in web development with Angular and TypeScript, and has been working with Angular for several years in multiple contexts (consulting, start-ups, and contracting) and countries (Spain, Ireland, and France), which has added professional value and experience to his career.

Alejandro is also an organizer of the GDG Seville, where he organizes meetups about Angular, TypeScript, and NestJS. He is currently working remotely for a multinational corporation based in USA as an Angular developer.

> *Thanks to my friends and family for their support and patience during those long working days. Especially to Monica, my girlfriend, who always has a smile for me and for being by my side throughout my career.*

Packt is searching for authors like you

If you're interested in becoming an author for Packt, please visit `authors.packtpub.com` and apply today. We have worked with thousands of developers and tech professionals, just like you, to help them share their insight with the global tech community. You can make a general application, apply for a specific hot topic that we are recruiting an author for, or submit your own idea.

Table of Contents

Preface — 1

Chapter 1: Getting Started with TypeScript — 7
  Grunt — 8
  Gulp — 10
  Webpack — 12
  NPM/CLI — 14
  TypeScript compiler — 15
    Files location — 16
      rootDir and outDir — 16
      baseUrl and paths — 16
      sourceRoot and sourceMap and mapRoot — 17
      Files and include and exclude — 18
      Outfile — 18
    Type — 19
      typeRoots and types — 19
      Declaration and declarationdir — 19
    Configuration file — 20
    Module and ModuleResolution — 21
    ECMAScript — 22
      Target — 23
      Lib — 23
    Compiler strictness — 23
      Strict — 24
      StrictFunctionTypes — 24
      StrictPropertyInitialization and StricNullChecks — 24
  Summary — 25

Chapter 2: Onboarding Types with Primitive — 27
  The difference between var, let, and const — 27
    Declaring with var — 28
    Declaring with let — 29
    const — 31
    Enhancing primitives with TypeScript — 31
      Number — 32
    String — 33
    Boolean — 34
    Null — 35
    Undefined — 36
    Symbol — 37
    Non-primitive — 38
      What is void? — 39

Table of Contents

The reasons to avoid using any type	40
Usage of the never type	40
Unknown type to have a stricter any type	42
Enforcing a type in a list	42
Defining a conscribed set of constants with enum	43
String literal and its difference compared to a string	46
Crafting a typed function	48
How to be strongly typed without specifying the type	**51**
Summary	**53**
Chapter 3: Unleashing the Power of Type with Objects	**55**
How to strongly type a set/dictionary with an index signature	**56**
TypeScript and map	**59**
The differences between index signature and a map	**60**
The differences between object and Object	**61**
When to use object, Object, or any	**62**
What is an object literal?	**63**
How to create a constructed object	**64**
The differences between an explicit type and a cast	**64**
Variable with many types	**65**
Combining type with intersect	**66**
Intersecting with something other than a type	**68**
Intersecting with an optional type	**68**
Merge type with inheritance	**69**
The differences between type and interface	**69**
Destructuring a type and an array	**70**
Tuple	**72**
The differences between declare and let/const/var	**74**
Summary	**75**
Chapter 4: Transforming Your Code into Object-Oriented	**77**
What is a class and how do we define one?	**78**
How type comes into play with a class's constructor	**78**
What is encapsulation using public, private, and protected	**80**
Reducing the definition of a field with a value set at construction time	**81**
What is static?	**82**
Use cases for a non-public constructor	**83**
Using an object from a class versus an object literal	**84**
How an interface can be useful in object-oriented	**87**
Bringing abstraction with an abstract class	**88**
How to have a property that is read-only	**90**
Enforcing a specific constructor from an interface	**92**
Summary	**93**

Chapter 5: Scoping Variables with Different Patterns — 95
- Comparing at runtime and design time with typeof — 96
- Differentiating undefined from null — 97
- Getting the type of element in a union — 97
- The limitations of instanceof — 98
- Using of a discriminator for type identification — 100
- The user-defined guard pattern — 102
- The reason to cast a type — 104
- What is a type assertion? — 106
- Comparing classes — 108
- Narrowing type for function with a union in signatures — 111
- Summary — 112

Chapter 6: Reusing Code Through Generic — 113
- Generic code to increase reusability — 113
- Accepted kinds of data structure for generic type — 115
- Constaining a generic type — 116
- Generic and intersection — 118
- Default generic — 119
- Generic optional type — 120
- Generic constraints with a union type — 121
- Restricting string choices with keyof — 121
- Limiting the access to members of a generic type — 122
- Reducing your type creation with mapped type — 124
- Generic type in TSX File — 126
- Summary — 127

Chapter 7: Mastering the Art of Defining Types — 129
- How to use a third-party library definition file — 130
- How typescript can generate a definition file — 131
- How to manually add a definition file for a JavaScript project — 131
- How to merge types into an existing definition file — 132
- Creating a definition file for a JavaScript project — 134
  - Definition file for global structure library — 134
  - Definition file for module library — 136
- JavaScript library without a definition file — 138
- Using another module from a definition file — 138
- Adding a definition file to an extension of an existing module — 138
- Summary — 139

Other Books You May Enjoy — 141

Index — 145

Preface

This quick start guide is a book that covers every topic related to TypeScript. This book takes the reader through all the features and benefits of using TypeScript. With this guide, you will grow your typing skills, which will make your JavaScript knowledge in play. TypeScript is a superset of JavaScript. This book does not teach you how to do web programming but illustrates how to use TypeScript on top of a language that you already know and like.

Who this book is for

This book is for developers who know JavaScript but have never touched Typescript.

What this book covers

`Chapter 1`, *Getting Started with TypeScript*, covers how to bring TypeScript into a new project or an existing JavaScript project. We will see how to set up your environment in your current build setup. TypeScript is supported by a variety of build tools, such as Grunt, Gulp, Webpack, or simply using the CLI. We also dive into the essential options, among all the ones that are available, to help you get started with TypeScript.

`Chapter 2`, *Onboarding Types with Primitive,* illustrates scoping a variable, the subtlety between undefined variables and null variables, and how to make a variable optional or required. At the end of this chapter, the reader will be in a situation where all the variables will be declared properly with an type that's accurate supported by TypeScript. The distinction between a primitive and non-primitive type will not be a conundrum anymore. The use of enum or symbol will be natural, and the creation of new types will become a habit any time a new domain object is introduced in your system.

`Chapter 3`, *Unleashing the Power of Type with Objects,* illustrates the difference between an object, Object, object literal and an object built with a constructor. This chapter also introduces the notion of a union between types that will allow an infinite combination of types for a single value. Furthermore, the concept of intersection is introduced, which allows us to manipulate type differently. At the end of this chapter, the reader will be able to create complex combinations of objects that hold advanced structures. We will dissect how to create a dictionary with a strongly typed index signature, understand how type can be beneficial with a map, and how to use the right object in order to be as accurate as possible when defining an object that can have a broad reach.

Chapter 4, *Transforming Your Code in Object-Oriented*, explains that object-oriented programming has its own set of terminology, and TypeScript relies on many of them. In this chapter, all the concepts of object-oriented programming that TypeScript supports are discussed with examples. We will see what a class is and how to instantiate a class into an object. In the same vein, we will see how a constructor can be strongly typed with TypeScript, but also how with a shorthand syntax we can assign a class's fields directly from the constructor. The principle of encapsulation with visibility, how to implement an interface, and how to bring abstraction to a class are all covered.

Chapter 5, *Scoping Variables with Different Patterns*, covers the subtlety the most basic concept, which is the variable. Knowing the exact type from a primitive to an object is essential for accessing specific members. Scoping down the exact type at runtime and design time is crucial for consistency between the two environments and to have feedback about what is possible or not. The variety of configuration among the different types of variable requires many different patterns that are covered in this chapter.

Chapter 6, *Reusing Code through Generic*, builds on ideas introduced in the previous chapters. The chapter builds these ideas by enhancing type and making them generic. Basic topics, such as defining a generic class and interface, are present. Through the chapter, we move into more advanced topics, such as generic constraints. The goal of this chapter is to make your code more generic to increase the reusability of your classes, functions, and structures to reduce the burden of duplicating code.

Chapter 7, *Mastering the Art of Defining Types*, covers how to create type from libraries that we are not working directly with but by importing the library inside your TypeScript project. The main difference is that when consuming code outside your project, you will not directly use TypeScript code but their definition. The reason is that JavaScript is provided in those libraries, not TypeScript code. We will see how it is possible to master the art of creating definition files for code that does not provide them, allowing you to keep working in a strong environment.

To get the most out of this book

This book is for JavaScript developers who want to get started with TypeScript for building applications. No previous knowledge of TypeScript is expected.

Download the example code files

You can download the example code files for this book from your account at `www.packtpub.com`. If you purchased this book elsewhere, you can visit `www.packtpub.com/support` and register to have the files emailed directly to you.

Preface

You can download the code files by following these steps:

1. Log in or register at `www.packtpub.com`.
2. Select the **SUPPORT** tab.
3. Click on **Code Downloads & Errata**.
4. Enter the name of the book in the **Search** box and follow the onscreen instructions.

Once the file is downloaded, please make sure that you unzip or extract the folder using the latest version of:

- WinRAR/7-Zip for Windows
- Zipeg/iZip/UnRarX for Mac
- 7-Zip/PeaZip for Linux

The code bundle for the book is also hosted on GitHub at `https://github.com/PacktPublishing/Typescript-3.0-Quick-Start-Guide`. In case there's an update to the code, it will be updated on the existing GitHub repository.

We also have other code bundles from our rich catalog of books and videos available at `https://github.com/PacktPublishing/`. Check them out!

Download the color images

We also provide a PDF file that has color images of the screenshots/diagrams used in this book. You can download it here: `https://www.packtpub.com/sites/default/files/downloads/TypeScript3QuickStartGuide_ColorImages.pdf`.

Conventions used

There are a number of text conventions used throughout this book.

`CodeInText`: Indicates code words in text, database table names, folder names, filenames, file extensions, pathnames, dummy URLs, user input, and Twitter handles. Here is an example: "Mount the downloaded `WebStorm-10*.dmg` disk image file as another disk in your system."

A block of code is set as follows:

```
let a:number = 2;
a = "two"; // Doesn't compile
```

When we wish to draw your attention to a particular part of a code block, the relevant lines or items are set in bold:

```
function switchFunction(num: number) {
    let b: string = "functionb";

    switch (num) {
        case 1:
            let b: string = "case 1";
            break;
    }
}
```

Bold: Indicates a new term, an important word, or words that you see onscreen. For example, words in menus or dialog boxes appear in the text like this. Here is an example: "Select **System info** from the **Administration** panel."

Warnings or important notes appear like this.

Tips and tricks appear like this.

Get in touch

Feedback from our readers is always welcome.

General feedback: Email `feedback@packtpub.com` and mention the book title in the subject of your message. If you have questions about any aspect of this book, please email us at `questions@packtpub.com`.

Errata: Although we have taken every care to ensure the accuracy of our content, mistakes do happen. If you have found a mistake in this book, we would be grateful if you would report this to us. Please visit www.packtpub.com/submit-errata, selecting your book, clicking on the Errata Submission Form link, and entering the details.

Piracy: If you come across any illegal copies of our works in any form on the Internet, we would be grateful if you would provide us with the location address or website name. Please contact us at copyright@packtpub.com with a link to the material.

If you are interested in becoming an author: If there is a topic that you have expertise in and you are interested in either writing or contributing to a book, please visit authors.packtpub.com.

Reviews

Please leave a review. Once you have read and used this book, why not leave a review on the site that you purchased it from? Potential readers can then see and use your unbiased opinion to make purchase decisions, we at Packt can understand what you think about our products, and our authors can see your feedback on their book. Thank you!

For more information about Packt, please visit packtpub.com.

Getting Started with TypeScript

In this chapter, we will look at TypeScript and see how to use TypeScript in a new project or an existing JavaScript project. We will see how to adapt the environment of your current build setup. TypeScript can be supported by a variety of build tools, such as Grunt, Gulp, webpack, or simply by using the **command-line interface** (**CLI**). We also look at the best options, among all the ones available, for getting started with TypeScript.

Before configuring any build tool, it's important to understand that all of them use the same TypeScript compiler, often called a transpiler. The TypeScript compiler is available by using npm:

```
npm install -g typescript
```

Npm might not be installed by default on your computer. If that is the case, the previous instruction will fail. It means you need to install Node.js. You can install Node.js by going to the official website, `https://nodejs.org/`.

At any time, you can verify that you have Node.js, npm, and TypeScript installed by using the following command:

```
node -v
npm -v
tsc -v
```

TSC is the executable for the TypeScript compiler. This is the one that is used by all build tools. Grunt, Gulp, and webpack use TSC via their own plugin infrastructures that map TSC features to their platform. Note that recent TSC features might take a few weeks before reaching these platforms. This might explain the differences in compiler options when using these three build systems. In contrast, using a TSC CLI ensures that you are using TypeScript directly.

Getting Started with TypeScript

This chapter covers the following:

- Grunt
- Gulp
- Webpack
- NMP/CLI
- TypeScript compiler

Grunt

Grunt is a JavaScript task runner. It can be installed using NPM, which is used to list all its plugins:

```
npm install -g grunt-cli
```

In the case of a new project, make sure that `package.json` exists in the root of your TypeScript project. You can generate a simple one by using `npm init`.

Once it is done, you can install Grunt into your project:

```
npm install grunt --save-dev
```

Once Grunt is available on your machine and specified in your project, you need to get a TypeScript plugin. Grunt has two plugins named `grunt -TypeScript` and `grunt-TS`. The former has not been maintained for a few years and lacks the latest TypeScript compiler configuration. I strongly suggest using the latter:

```
npm install grunt-ts --save-dev
```

The last package should be installed as a dev dependency for Grunt to compile TypeScript and to install it locally. Grunt will search for the package locally. Omitting TypeScript as a local dependency will result in the following error when executing Grunt.

 **ENOENT**: no such file or directory, open '/.../node_modules/grunt-ts/node_modules/typescript/package.json' Use `--force` to continue.

Installing TypeScript locally as a `dev` dependency is easy:

```
npm install typescript --save-dev
```

[8]

Prior to `grunt-ts` version 6, TypeScript and Grunt were installed during the installation of `grunt-ts`. This is not the case anymore, so they must be added manually.

The next step is to configure Grunt to use a TypeScript plugin. If you are not using Grunt, you need to create a `Gruntfile.js` at the root of your project. Otherwise, you can edit your existing one. The plugin allows you to specify many TypeScript options in the `Gruntfile.js`, but a good practice is to limit TypeScript options directly in the file and to leverage the TypeScript configuration file. By configuring TypeScript outside Grunt, this gives you the possibility of compiling your code without Grunt, or migrating to another build tool without having to duplicate or change TypeScript preferences.

A minimalist Grunt configuration with the sole purpose of compiling TypeScript into JavaScript may look like the following:

```
module.exports = function(grunt) {
  grunt.initConfig({
    ts: {
      default : {
        tsconfig: './tsconfig.json'
      }
    }
  });
  grunt.loadNpmTasks("grunt-ts");
  grunt.registerTask("default", ["ts"]);
};
```

The Grunt configuration creates a default task that executes a custom `ts` task that links to the `tsconfig.json` file, which is the default TypeScript configuration file.

The `tsconfig.json` file can look like the following one, which takes every TypeScript file with the extension `.ts` and will compile them outputting the result in the `build` folder:

```
{
  "compilerOptions": {
    "rootDir": "src",
    "outDir": "build",
  }
}
```

When using `grunt` and `grunt-ts`, you must ensure that that the JSON is valid with no-trailing commas in the `tsconfig.json` file. Otherwise, you may get the following error:

```
tsconfig error: "Error parsing \"./tsconfig.json\". It may not be valid JSON in UTF-8."
```

Getting Started with TypeScript

To test the configuration, create a simple `index.ts` file in an `src` folder at the root of the project. You can type `console.log('test')`. After, run `grunt` in a command line at the root of your project as well. This will create a `build` folder with an `index.js` file containing the same line of code. It will also create the `js.map` file that will let you debug in your browser directly in TypeScript's code.

If, for some reason, you do not want to rely on `tsconfig.json`, it's possible to specify the source and destination directly into `Gruntfile.js` file:

```
module.exports = function (grunt) {
  grunt.initConfig({
    ts: {
      default: {
        src: ["src/**/*.ts"],
        outDir: "build",
        options: {
          rootDir: "src"
        }
      }
    }
  });
  grunt.loadNpmTasks("grunt-ts");
  grunt.registerTask("default", ["ts"]);
};
```

In the end, `grunt-ts` wraps the TypeScript command line. It provides options such as the *fast compilation*, which compile, only what has changed since the last compilation. It is also an interesting option if you are already using Grunt in your project and want to start using TypeScript without modifying your build process.

Gulp

Gulp is an automation toolkit that has a TypeScript plugin as well. There are two plugins available in NPM, which are `gulp-tsb` and `gulp-typescript`. The latter is the most popular and more maintained. You can fetch `gulp` and the plugin by using the following command:

```
npm install -g gulp
npm install --save-dev gulp-typescript
```

If you do not have a Gulp configuration file, you will need to create one at the root of your `gulpfile.js` project.

The configuration without an explicit option will rely on the default configuration. It means that configuring Gulp can be as simple as piping the source into the TypeScript plugin and then piping the result into the destination folder where the `build` files, that is the JavaScript file, will be placed for consumption. Once the following code is placed in `gulpfile.js`, you can execute it by using `gulp` in the command line. This will execute the *default task* once, automatically:

```
var gulp = require("gulp");
var ts = require("gulp-typescript");

gulp.task("default", function () {
 var tsResult = gulp.src("src/**/*.ts")
 .pipe(ts());
 return tsResult.js.pipe(gulp.dest("build"));
});
```

It is possible to have a task in Gulp to build incrementally a TypeScript file that changes instead of building all of them. This can be useful on a big project to reduce the time between the edition and the access to the result. This is similar to the *fast compilation* of Grunt. To have an ongoing compilation, you must create a new Gulp task. In this example, we will change Gulp to rely on `tsconfig.json` file, which will allow us to separate the TypeScript compiler option from the Gulp configuration:

```
var gulp = require('gulp');
var ts = require('gulp-typescript');
var tsProject = ts.createProject('tsconfig.json');

gulp.task('scripts', function() {
 return gulp.src('src/**/*.ts')
 .pipe(tsProject())
 .pipe(gulp.dest('build'));
});
gulp.task('watch', ['scripts'], function() {
 gulp.watch('src/**/*.ts', ['scripts']);
});
```

To run the `watch` task, you need to execute Gulp followed by the name of the task: `gulp watch`. Unlike Grunt, Gulp will not produce the `map` file. It requires an additional Gulp plugin. Because the sourceMap is crucial to have an efficient debugging environment, it is keen to download the `gulp-sourcemap` package and change the previous configuration to the following. But first, let's download the `gulp-sourcemaps` package:

```
npm install --save-dev gulp-sourcemaps
```

And then create a new task:

```
var sourcemaps = require('gulp-sourcemaps');
gulp.task('scriptswithsourcemap', function () {
 return gulp.src('src/**/*.ts')
 .pipe(sourcemaps.init())
 .pipe(tsProject())
 .pipe(sourcemaps.write('.', { includeContent: false, sourceRoot: '.'}))
 .pipe(gulp.dest('build'));
});
```

The configuration will create the source map in a file with the same name as the JavaScript file generated but with a different extension. The extension will be `.jsmap`. If you want to have the mapping directly in the JavaScript file, you can remove the two arguments passed in the `write` function. I suggest having a single script task that produces the source map in a file to separate the mapping from the code generated, and to always have the source map created. It's a small tax on the compilation and a huge gain in debugging.

Webpack

Webpack is one of the most commonly used ways to automate workflow when working with JavaScript and web development. Its main purpose is to bundle, but it can do many sequential steps, such as compiling TypeScript. Similarly to Grunt and Gulp, webpack has two loaders (similar to a plugin) for TypeScript. One is called `ts-loader` and the second `awesome-typescript-loader`. While with Grunt and Gulp, it was a clear which one users prefer, this is not the case with Webpack. Both loaders are similar in terms of popularity. It is also not difficult to change between the two if needed. Originally, `awesome-typescript-loader` was faster than `ts-loader` but with the evolution of TypeScript, the difference is often minimal. Also, there is sometimes an issue with an advanced feature in one or the other, and so it is practical to be able to switch depending on how your project. I'll present `ts-loader`, which is a little more popular, still actively maintained, and has a little more usage than the `awesome-typescript-loader`.

In the case, you are not yet using `webpack`, we need to install it:

```
npm install --save-dev webpack
npm install --save-dev webpack-cli
```

Once webpack is installed, you can install the TypeScript loader:

```
npm install --save-dev ts-loader
```

Once all the tools are installed, you can configure webpack to bundle the JavaScript produced by the `webpack` loader. However, `webpack.config.js` is needed at the root of your project. Like any Webpack configuration, the entry property must be defined. Make sure you are referring to the TypeScript file. The output is also specified in the output property. Webpack requires mentioning the extension to be analyzed. In TypeScript case it is `.ts`, but if you are working with React you might want to also add `.tsx` under `resolve:extensions`. Finally, the `ts-loader` is specified under `module:rules`. Once again, the extension of TypeScript is required and the name of the loader:

```
module.exports = {
  mode: "development",
  devtool: "source-map",
  entry: "./src/index.ts",
  output: {
   path: __dirname + "/build",
   filename: "bundle.js"
  },
  resolve: {
   extensions: [".ts"]
  },
  module: {
   rules: [
   { test: /\.ts$/, loader: "ts-loader" }
   ]
  }
};
```

You can run the webpack command line (`cli`) by accessing the binary file, which will read the `webpack.config.js` file:

```
node node-modules/webpack-cli/bin/cli.js
```

If you want to avoid referencing `node_modules`, you can install `webpack-cli` in your global space, using `npm install -g webpack-cli`.

Here are a few little details about webpack. There is an additional module that divides the production of the bundle and compilation, compared to just validating TypeScript. These modules might be interesting when your project starts to grow and you want to have a faster compilation pace. Feel free to check `fork-ts-checker-webpack-plugin` and `thread-loader`. Before diving into other libraries, `ts-loader` has a way to incrementally build and to use the TypeScript watch API to avoid building everything all the time. This will increase your performance on every compilation. To allow the watch, change the rule of `ts-loader` to the following:

```
rules: [
 {
 test: /\.ts$/,
 use: [
  {
   loader: 'ts-loader',
   options: {
    transpileOnly: true,
    experimentalWatchApi: true,
   },
  },
 ],
 }
]
```

A final detail about webpack is its dependency on `tsconfig.json` for all TypeScript related configurations. Grunt and Gulp allow you to override configurations inside their tool configuration, which is not the case with webpack. When bundling, webpack produces `bundle.js.map`, but only if the dev tool specifies a configuration. However, you must set the `tsconfig.json` "sourceMap" to `true` to have a mapping that works with TypeScript.

NPM/CLI

Almost all web projects use NPM. NPM is the mechanism we used to fetch TypeScript. This one creates `package.json` at the root of your project and can be used to launch TypeScript directly. This is possible because TypeScript has a CLI called **tsc** (**TypeScript compiler**).

NPM configuration has a section named `scripts` where you can add any command you want. You can create a `build` one that invokes tsc. Without any parameters, tsc uses `tsconfig.json` at the root of your project. In the following snippet, the "build" script is defined. To run the command, the use of the `run` command of NPM is needed, that is, `npm run build`:

```
"scripts": {
"build": "node_modules/typescript/bin/tsc"
},
```

With a TypeScript configuration file that specifies the source map, the `rootDir`, and `outDir` the result will be the same as Gulp and Grunt (different from webpack since it won't be bundled):

```
{
 "compilerOptions": {
 "rootDir": "src",
 "outDir": "build",
 "sourceMap": true
 }
}
```

This is often not the preferred configuration because of how simplistic and limited it is. However, it's possible to have several commands executed one after the other, using the double ampersand (`&&`) to create a chain of commands. This option is fast, doesn't require any dependency on NPM libraries, and is often enough to get started at a basic level.

The advantage of the NPM and CLI approach is that TypeScript can be executed easily. Hence, if you have a custom build system you can easily plug TypeScript by invoking the CLI.

TypeScript compiler

Considering all the tooling available to compile TypeScript to JavaScript, one pillar concept remains the same: you must know which configuration to use. Insofar that you are not responsible for configuring the compiler, you could skip this section – configuring TypeScript is something you do rarely and when it works as desired it can stay unaltered for a very long time. However, to have an understanding of the capability of TypeScript, you need to know some of the core options. In this section, we will see the main settings that you can enable and customize for your project.

Files location

This section is all about the configuration of files in the file system. It guides TypeScript on where to find different files in your machine, as well as where to generate JavaScript files.

rootDir and outDir

The most basic configuration that you need to set for your project is to indicate to TypeScript where to get TypeScript files and where to publish the result of the compilation. Where will be the TypeScript (`.ts`) files and the JavaScript (`.js`) files be produced. This is done by specifying `rootDir` and `outDir`. Avoiding `rootDir` might give you a surprise in `outDir`. By default, TypeScript computes what it should be and tries to find a common path, which is the longest common prefix of all your input files. That has the drawback of being inconsistent when the file structures change. Recently, TypeScript changed its behavior to have a default to `.`, which alleviate the issue. Nevertheless, having an explicit configuration is the best practice to avoid confusion as to which version of TypeScript this new rule was applied.

Example:

```
rootDir:src
outDir:build
```

baseUrl and paths

Confusion can arise when the baseUrl and paths come into play. The baseUrl allows specifying with a non-relative name to be resolved. Paths work closely with the baseUrl and is a map of key-value allowing a name to be used as a link to a specific path to the library, using the baseUrl as the root.

Here is an example:

```
{
 "compilerOptions": {
 "baseUrl": ".", // This must be specified if "paths" is.
 "paths": {
 "jquery": ["node_modules/jquery/dist/jquery"] // This mapping is relative to "baseUrl"
 }
 }
}
```

In code:

```
Import * from "jquery"
```

Paths can also be used for more advanced scenarios where you can define fallback folders. As good practice, I would advise using a relative path as much as possible and avoid complicated structures and potential resolving issues.

sourceRoot and sourceMap and mapRoot

The sourceMap property is a boolean that when set to `true` will generate the mapping between the generated JavaScript and TypeScript. This is a good option to turn on if you do debug in a browser and want to step in the TypeScript code instead of stepping into the generated code. It simplifies the debugging because you are working in exactly the same area. This is most of the time turned on.

However, sourceRoot is rarely used in normal circumstances. It is available if you move the sourceMap somewhere else to indicate at runtime where to find the sourceMap. This will alter the generated sourceMap path. The following code shows a comment indicating the path of the map file. SourceRoot would change the portion before `index.js.map`:

```
const text = "Text for test1";
console.log(text);
//# sourceMappingURL=index.js.map
```

Similarly, mapRoot allows changing the source if the map files are in a different place than the JavaScript file. The difference between sourceRoot and mapRoot is this time we alter the map file instead of the JavaScript file. In the following partial extraction of a code of a map file, we see paths that can be modified by mapRoot:

```
{"version":3,"file":"index.js","sourceRoot":"","sources":["../src/index.ts"
]......
```

The moment to use or the other depending on how you configure positions your built files. If you move the map somewhere else, then `sourceRoot` is interesting. However, if you keep the map but move the JavaScript somewhere else than you may change mapRoot. I mention these configurations for the sole reason that you may already have a JavaScript project that you want to migrate to TypeScript. Depending on your existing configuration, you may need to tweak these configurations. However, for any standard project, no modification should be made to these configurations.

Files and include and exclude

Included is an array that specifies the glob pattern that in turn specifies which files/folders are to be included in the compilation. The array `exclude` complements `include` and removes files to be compiled. When both properties are specified, `exclude` will filter out from the list included files from `include`. By default, `include` includes all TypeScript files under the `rootDir`, hence no need to add an entry to `**/*.ts`.

Files are rarely used because it is less flexible than `include`. It allows specifying by path and name which file to compile, instead of using a glob pattern. The pattern approach is more flexible allowing you to configure once instead of having to continually modify the configuration file by adding and removing entries in Files.

Here is an example:

```
"include": [
"src/**/*"
],
"exclude": [
"node_modules",
"dont/compile/*.mock.ts"
]
```

A final word on these three file configurations is that, contrary to most options, these ones don't reside under `compilerOptions` but are directly set at the root of the `tsconfig.json` file.

Outfile

The outfile is an option that can be useful if you have a need to generate a single JavaScript file from many TypeScript files. When using the outfile, you can remove `outDir` and set a path relative to the root of your project, followed with the name and the extension of the generated file:

```
{
 "compilerOptions": {
 "rootDir": "src",
 "outDir": "build",
 "target": "es6",
 "sourceMap": true,
 "outFile": "build/mySingleFile.js"
 }
}
```

The example code above creates a single file but also the `sourceMap` file because of the `sourceMap`.

Type

This section contains information about TypeScript's type. The first configuration gives TypeScript a hint as to where to look for types and also if TypeScript must generate the definition file or not when compiling.

typeRoots and types

By default, every type provided inside a `node_modules` library, which includes all specific `@types/` and package with `.d.ts` directly inside the library's folder, are read by the TypeScript compiler. However, in some scenarios where there is no definition file available and you need to provide a custom one then you need to specify where the definition file is located. This can be done by using in which you can specify a folder where you define all your definition files. The caveat is that you will need to specify `node_modules` if you want TypeScript to keep look for definition files in `node_modules`.

```
{
 "compilerOptions": {
 "typeRoots" : ["./typings", "./node_modules"]
 }
}
```

The Types configuration allows cherry-picking which file TypeScript will include. It works in collaboration with typeRoots and is an array. It whitelists the type name.

Declaration and declarationdir

If you are building a library instead of a website or program, it might be wise to provide the definition file along with the generated JavaScript file. The reason is that when building a library in TypeScript, we never share the actual TypeScript (`.ts`) files but instead share the JavaScript files. The rationale is that TypeScript is just a superset of JavaScript and we want to expose our code to the largest audience available. By providing the JavaScript files we are allowing every JavaScript developer to consume our work. However, TypeScript coders are at rest. To fix this issue, we can provide a definition file (`.d.ts`) that contains all the signature functions as well as exported variables. The TypeScript compiler lets you generate the definition file automatically by using `declaration`.

The option is `boolean`:

```
{
  "compilerOptions": {
    "declaration" : true
  }
}
```

By default, the declaration files produced are by TypeScript file and located at the same place as the TypeScript file. It means that the end result is for each JavaScript (`.js`) you will see a brother declaration file (`.d.ts`) next to it:

```
{
  "compilerOptions": {
    "declaration" : true,
    "declarationDir": "definitionfiles/here"
  }
}
```

There is a caveat with `declarationDir`, which is that it cannot be used with `outFile`. You will get a compilation-error mentioning that both options cannot be defined at the same time:

```
error TS5053: Option 'declarationDir' cannot be specified with option 'outFile'.
```

Configuration file

TypeScript has its own configuration file that is a convenient way to avoid passing every option by command-line arguments. The file resides at the root of your project. One possibility is to have several configuration files that can be used in different situations. This is possible by providing **tsc** with the option -p followed by the name of the configuration. The following three command-line invocations show one without any parameter, which is doing exactly the same compilation as the second line. Nonetheless, the third compilation instruction is different, pointing to a completely new set of options:

```
tsc
tsc -p tsconfig.json
tsc -p tsconfig.test.json
```

One benefit of configuration files is the possibility of reusability by extending configuration. You can see this principle like object-oriented inheritance – one file can inherit from another one. This can be done by using the `extends` property as a key and the file to inherit from as a value. The file provided must be relative to the root of your project.It can or not have the extension (`.json`):

```
{
  "extends": "./tsconfig.json",
  "compilerOptions": {
  "outDir": "buildtest",
  "sourceMap": false,
  "declaration": false
  }
}
```

The following example shows a command that invokes a compilation with the option in `tsconfig.test.json` and has a small set of instructions:

```
tsc -p tsconfig.test.json
```

The first one is which file to extend. In that case, it could also have been `./tsconfig` without the extension. The file overrides `outDir` that is also provided in the `tsconfig.json` file and adds additional values. A good pattern is to have a `base` configuration, which has a configuration that you know will be shared across many of your configurations.

Module and ModuleResolution

A key concept of code separation in JavaScript is a module. A module brings the notion of importing and exporting code. The capability increases the ability to share the code by specifying a specific name and which part of a code may be exported. Then, other software can import the code and leverage its functionalities. However, there is not a single way to craft a module. TypeScript lets you write your code in a single way and to produce, during compilation, an output that respects different popular module syntax. Here is a list of modules that TypeScript can interpret:

```
"None", "CommonJS", "AMD", "System", "UMD", "ES6", "ES2015" or "ESNext".
```

The `module` option can be seen as how TypeScript produces the module and `moduleResolution` as how it reads a module. There are two ways that TypeScript can understand an `import` statement: class and node. The former is the traditional TypeScript way, which has different rules to find a file that is imported. The more popular choice is `node`.

Regardless of the module resolution option, you should try to use relative resolution by specifying in your import a path from the file you are importing. Relative import is denoted by having a path that starts with a single dot or a double dot to move backward. Here are few relative imports:

```
import x from "./sameFolder";
import y from "../parent/folder";
import z from "../../../deeper/";
```

The reason for using this is the clarity of where the code is imported. Using the absolute resolution brings confusion because it relies on other configurations like `baseUrl` as well as `moduleResolution`.

On the contrary, an import that relies on a more complex resolution is non-relative and looks like the following:

```
import a from "module123";
```

Without going into all the complex rules, the last example in classic would look for the module next to the file that is importing it and go down the folder structure without trying to import the module from `node_modules`. However, if `moduleResolution` is set to `node` than the first check would be to look-up in the `node_modules` folder for a `module123`. As you see, if you are using a common name, you may load an unexpected module.

ECMAScript

This section contains Typescript configurations related to the type of ECMAScript produced, as well as additional packages that can be incorporated.

Target

The target option must be specified but rarely changed. This option indicates to TypeScript which version of the JavaScript files to produce. By default, it produces an ECMAScript 3 version, which doesn't have all the built-in features that TypeScript allows. However, TypeScript can still produce such old versions of ECMAScript by producing JavaScript code that mimics the features. This comes with a price of performance penalty at runtime, but it is a great way to build modern code with an older browser. Here is the actual target that you can specify:

```
"ES3", "ES5", "ES6"/"ES2015", "ES2016", "ES2017" or "ESNext"
```

If you are deploying for the web in general, ES5 is a safe bet with 100% support for all browsers. But, ES6 is very close, and Chrome supports 98% of its features, Firefox 97%, and Edge 96%.

Lib

TypeScript can inject the core library of ECMAScript into the produced code. By default, some libraries are automatically added. For example, if you specify a target of ES5, TypeScript adds the library: DOM, ES5, and ScriptHost. You can manually add an additional library. For example, if you would like to use iterable you can add the string `ES2015.Iterable` in the lib array. You can use a feature that is beyond your main target as well. For example, you can have a target of ES2015 and uses an ES2018 feature. See "target" as a main set of features to be included in the compilation and `lib` as a subset of additional features that you can add to the compilation.

Compiler strictness

TypeScript has many option around how strict the compiler must analyze your code. This section shows you the difference between each setting, allowing you to start slowly and progressively if you are coming from an existing JavaScript.

Strict

This is the option that turns every configuration to strict. This is what you should use if you start a new TypeScript project coming from JavaScript.

StrictFunctionTypes

This is an advanced check that does not allow bivariance for arguments of a function. It uses contravariance. What it means is that if a function is expecting a type A as a parameter, you cannot set a function that has a type B that inherits a type A – you must only pass a type A. The following won't compile with `StrictFunctionTypes` with a `true` value. The strict option is useful to avoid a passing object that has more members than the expected type. The following example has B as the `firstName` field and inherits A, hence the name:

```
interface A {
 name: string;
}

interface B extends A {
 firstName: string;
}

declare let f1: (x: A) => void;
declare let f2: (x: B) => void;

f1 = f2; // DOESNT COMPILE
f2 = f1;
```

During compilation, TypeScript finds that the argument is passed to an object with more members and won't compile:

```
Error message : Type 'A' is not assignable to type 'B'. Property
'firstName' is missing in type 'A'.
```

StrictPropertyInitialization and StricNullChecks

`StrictPropertyInitialization` property should always be set to true. It ensures that all properties of a class are initialized with a direct association at the declaration level or in the constructor of the class.

```
class A {
 public field1: number;
}
```

The example does not compile because `Field1` is a number that is not defined. The value of the field is undefined. There are many solutions to keep the strictness and make the code compliant. The first solution is to set a value at the initialization:

```
class A {
  public field1: number = 1;
}
```

Setting a default value at initialization is not always possible. In some cases, it's possible to specify the value at construction type:

```
class A {
  public field1: number;
  constructor(p:number){
    This.field1 = p;
  }
}
```

A third way to compile the code is to use the bang operator (`!`) after the member's name. The operator indicates to TypeScript that the value will be provided later. The scenario in which a late initialization occurs is often by some injection framework or by using a function to initialize the class.

One caveat to having `strictPropertyInitialization` do this job is a dependency on another strict property that must be enabled – the `strictNullChecks`. The null check should also always be set to true at all times. Without this, a field identified as a type will automatically accept null and undefined as a valid type. It is less confusing and more declarative to only support a field with an explicit type and in the case of null or/and undefined to use the property definition that we will see later in this book.

Summary

In this chapter, we put in place different configurations allowing you to start coding with TypeScript in a straightforward way. After setting up your working environment to your liking, we briefly mentioned the most important compiler options to get you started on the right path. TypeScript is a flexible compiler, and you should be rapidly up-to-speed developing because of how the settings can be selected.

In the next chapter, we will look at programming with TypeScript by introducing how ECMAScript primitive type can be strongly typed.

2
Onboarding Types with Primitive

Primitive types are all the basic supported categories of value. Each type represents a domain of values in which the integrity of the format is enforced. JavaScript has a limited set of primitives that can only be inferred by the assignation of a value to a variable. For example, a value can be a number, a date, a Boolean, a string, and so on. The assignation of a subsequent value of a different model to a singular variable is permitted. The side effect is the mutation of the type, which increases the complexity of any JavaScript program. TypeScript, however, can enforce type immutability, which reduces the risk of a potential wrong value that misleads the proper execution of the application. Also, TypeScript provides support on which operation can be used, depending on which explicit type is attached to a particular value. This chapter illustrates the scoping of a variable, the subtlety between an undefined variable and a null variable, and how to make a variable optional or required. At the end of this chapter, the reader will be in a situation where all the variables will be declared properly, with an accurate type supported by TypeScript. The distinction between a primitive and a non-primitive type will no longer be a conundrum. The use of `enum` or symbol will be natural and the creation of new types will become a habit any time a new domain object is introduced in your system.

This chapter will cover the following:

- The difference between `var`, `let`, and `const`
- How to be strongly typed without specifying the type

The difference between var, let, and const

TypeScript has many ways to declare a variable. You can define a variable at a function or global scope using one of the three following keywords: `var`, `let`, and `const`. Also, you can define a variable with `public`, `private`, or `protected` at the class level.

Declaring with var

The most basic way to declare a variable is by using the keyword `var`. It is the oldest declaration, but the least-preferred way because of some quirks. The main issue with `var` is that it gets declared in the execution context, which means inside the function scope or at the global scope. If, by accident a value is assigned to a variable not explicitly declared with `var`, then the scope of the variable is at the global scope. Here is an example:

```
function f1(){
   a = 2; // No explicit "var", hence global scope instead of function
   scope
}
```

A `var` declaration can be made stricter with the strict mode in JavaScript so that TypeScript can turn on every file automatically by using `alwaysStrict` in its compiler's options. Otherwise, you must remember that `var`–declared variables are created before the execution of the code. Variables without the keyword `var` do not exist until the code assigning them is executed. In JavaScript, it's possible to assign a variable without declaring, which is not the case with TypeScript:

```
a = 2; // Won't create a variable in TypeScript
```

While TypeScript can protect against an undeclared variable, it does not protect a `var` declaration against the side effect of **hoisting**. The issue comes from JavaScript, where a declaration with `var` is processed before other pieces of code, which brings the variable declaration to the top of the scope (function or global). The subtlety is that the declaration is moved up, but not the initialization. That being said, TypeScript will not let you use a variable defined under its usage:

```
console.log("Test", a); // Won't allow to use the variable in TypeScript
var a = 2;
```

Finally, `var` lets you define the variable that overrides the initial declaration or initialization more than once:

```
var a = 2;
var a = 23;
```

Chapter 2

Generally, the use of `var` is a dated way to declare a variable. With TypeScript, there is a big incentive to rely on `let` or `const` because you can generate an older ECMAScript version that will generate `var` but in a proper and valid format.

Declaring with let

A `let` declaration is scope-based. It cannot be declared more than once per scope, and it does not hoist the variable. It simplifies the readability of the code, and it avoids unexpected errors. Declaring with `let` also doesn't set any values globally. Relying on `let` is the way to declare a variable when you expect the variable to be set more than once. In the following code, the variable `a` is defined three times. The code is legal, even with several declarations. The reason is that each declaration, with `let`, is defined in a different scope with curly braces. The first scope is the function scope. The second scope uses an unusual syntax, but it reflects how a `while`, `if`, or other scope feature works. The third scope is within an `if` statement:

```
function letFunction() {
   let a: number = 1;
   { // Scope start
      let a: number = 2;
   } // Scope end
   console.log(a); // 1

   if(true){ // Scope start
      let a: number = 3;
   } // Scope end
   console.log(a); // 1
}
letFunction()
```

Furthermore, TypeScript ensures that once a declaration is done, the type associated with the variable is immutable. This means that a variable defined as a number will be a number for the rest of the lifespan of the variable:

```
let a:number = 2;
a = "two"; // Doesn't compile
```

Declaring a variable with `let` in a `switch` case can be tricky. The reason is the scoping is not by `case` but for the `switch` that hosts all the cases. However, it is possible to conceive a scope by summoning a curly bracket inside each `case`. The following code is valid even if two variables `b` are declared:

```
function switchFunction(num: number) {
```

[29]

Onboarding Types with Primitive

```
    let b: string = "functionb";

    switch (num) {
        case 1:
          let b: string = "case 1";
        break;
    }
}
```

However, adding a subsequent case that also declares a variable b fails the compilation:

```
function switchFunction(num: number) {
  let b: string = "functionb";

  switch (num) {
    case 1:
      let b: string = "case 1";
    break;
    case 2:
      let b: string = "case 2";
    break;
  }
}
```

The workaround for the default scope from the switch is to create an artificial scope for each case. The construction of the scope can be done by adding curly brackets, as shown in the following code:

```
function switchFunction(num: number) {
  let b: string = "functionb";

  switch (num) {
    case 1: {
      let b: string = "case 1";
    break;
    } // After break
    case 2: {
      let b: string = "case 2";
    } // Before break
    break;
  }

}
```

let is one of the most-used declarations and should always be used instead of var when const is not a valid option.

const

In the case where you know that the variable is set once and will not change, then using `const` is a better alternative. The reason is that it highlights to the reader of the code that the value cannot be set more than once—it is declared and initialized. TypeScript respects `let` and `const`, and the code will not compile if a variable is defined more than once or if a value is assigned twice when the variable is a constant.

Conscribing a variable to stay with a single value may look restrictive, but in many situations, it is the right thing to do. The declaration of a primitive with `const` blocks the access of assigning with the equals sign (=), which means that it does not allow you to change the reference of the variable. However, you can change the content of the variable. For example, an array of primitives can add and remove values from the array, but cannot assign a new list of values:

```
const arr: number[] = [1, 2, 3];
arr.push(4);
```

The following code shows that a member can be edited, even if the object is declared as a constant. However, the `myObj` is not assignable. It means that the reference will always remain the same:

```
const myObj: { x: number } = { x: 1 };
myObj.x = 2;
```

Finally, TypeScript, with the use of `let` and `const`, ensures that the value assigned to a variable is associated with the desired variable, and any faulty assignation will cause the compiler returning an error. In the following code, two variables are clearly defined at the global scope, as well as the function scope. There is no doubt that they are two distinct variables with any collusion of value:

```
const a = 2;
function z() {
    let a = 3;
}
```

Enhancing primitives with TypeScript

TypeScript has the same primitive variables as JavaScript. It is possible to declare a variable to hold a number, string, Boolean, and a symbol. Also, two primitives are available for a situation where no value is available: undefined and null. Finally, with these primitives, it's possible to have an array of each of them.

All primitives must use one declaration previously discussed with a unique variable name and use the colon followed by the word number. However, when used as a parameter of a function, the `declaration` keyword is avoided. There is no need to specify the scope of the variable because this one is for the function. The same goes for the visibility, which is only visible to the function receiving the parameter:

```
function noNeedConstLetvar(parameter1: number) { }
```

Number

TypeScript follows how JavaScript manipulates and carries the primitive type of a number by having a single type: number. A number can be an `integer`, a `float`, a `double`, negative, positive and even `NaN`.

A number cannot directly use a `boolean` value (neither `true`, neither `false`). A conversation by parsing the `boolean` is required:

```
let boolean: number = true; // Won't compile
```

There are many ways to convert a Boolean to a number. You can use the `Number` constructor that takes any value and converts it into a number of `1` for `true` and `0` for `false`:

```
let boolean1: number = Number(true);
let boolean2: number = Number(false);
```

You can use the ternary operator and manually select the desired value, which can be beyond `1` and `0`:

```
let boolean3: number = true ? 1 : 0;
let boolean4: number = false ? 1 : 0;
```

You can use the + sign to start an addition to the value, which automatically converts the `boolean` value to a number:

```
let boolean5: number = +true;
let boolean6: number = +false;
```

A number cannot use a string directly either. Many techniques borrowed from JavaScript are available. The first one is using `Number`, and similar to the `boolean` case will parse the string into a number:

```
let string1: number = Number("123.5");
let string2: number = Number("-123.5");
```

The second approach is using the `parseInt` function. The `parse` function has a second optional parameter that allows specifying the base. It is important to note that this should always be specified to avoid error with octal or hexadecimal:

```
let string3: number = parseInt("123.5", 10);
let string4: number = parseInt("-123.5", 10);
```

You can use the + sign to add to the value, which automatically converts the string value to a number:

```
let string5: number = +"123.5";
let string6: number = +"-123.5";
```

Converting a string into a number can be tricky if the string is written with **numeric separators**. A numeric separator allows writing a number in a human way by dividing the digit by an underscore. This increases the readability. For example, here are nine million one hundred:

```
let numeric_separator: number = 9_000_100;
```

Parsing a string with a numeric separator will fail, but this is also the case when using the `Number` approach as well as the + sign approach. The result is inconsistent and can be from `NaN` to parsing just the value before the first underscore. In that case, replacing all underscores and using one of the techniques previously mentioned would be the solution.

A number can be written in a different base. As in JavaScript, TypeScript uses the `0x` literal for hexadecimal, `0b` for binary, and `0o` for octal:

```
let number1: number = 0x10;
let number2: number = 0b10;
let number3: number = 0o10;
```

String

TypeScript is identical to JavaScript for a string. You can define a string between single quotes, double quotes, or backquotes. The single quote and double quote have the same function of assigning the string between the quotes to the variable:

```
let string1: string = 's1';
let string2: string = "s2";
let string3: string = `s3`;
```

Onboarding Types with Primitive

The backquote, or backtick, has a special name, **string interpolation**, which allows injecting code inside the string. This is possible using a special syntax with the dollar sign and curly brackets:

```
let interpolation1: string = `This contains the variable s1: ${string1} as well as ${string2}`;
let interpolation2: string = `Can invoke variable function: ${string1.substr(0, 1)} as well as any code like this addition: ${1 + 1}`;

console.log(interpolation2);
```

The last example produces this output: **Can invoke the variable function: s as well as any code like this addition: 2**.

Interpolation goes beyond just injecting other value and can run any TypeScript code. The previous example does an addition in the string. Another feature of string interpolation is that you can add a line break without having any compilation problem. With a single and a double quote, a string must be on the same line or be broken in several strings and concatenated with a + sign:

```
let multipleLine1: string = "Line1" +
    "Line2";

let multipleLine2: string = `Line1
    Line2`;
```

Boolean

A `boolean` type allows the lowercase `true` and `false` only. No number is authorized, neither different capitalization of the value. It's possible to convert a numeric value, that is `1` or `0`, by comparing it to `1`:

```
let bool1: boolean = true; // true
let bool2: boolean = false; // false
let bool3: boolean = 1 === 1; // true
```

It is also possible to use the JavaScript `Boolean` construction to have a conversion. TypeScript doesn't remove the quirks that come along with the parsing but returns a strongly typed `bool` value of the constructor. Here are some examples that barely any work for the case of a string with the value `false`:

```
let bool4: boolean = Boolean("true"); // true
let bool5: boolean = Boolean("TRUE"); // true
let bool6: boolean = Boolean("false"); // true
```

```
let bool7: boolean = Boolean("FALSE"); // true
let bool8: boolean = Boolean(NaN); // false

let bool9: boolean = new Boolean("true").valueOf(); // true
let bool10: boolean = new Boolean("false").valueOf(); // true

let bool11: boolean = "true" as any as boolean; // true
let bool12: boolean = "false" as any as boolean; // false
```

Only the last two lines are a TypeScript specific solution where we cast the string to type and then back to a `boolean`. It is also one of the only solutions that work, other than comparing to the string directly as shown in the following code:

```
let bool13 = isTrue("true"); // true
let bool14 = isTrue("false"); // false

function isTrue(s: string): boolean {
    return s.toLocaleLowerCase() === "true";
}
```

The preferred solution is to avoid casting to any. Casting opens the door to potential unexpected errors in most cases, even if in this particular situation, the casted value is controlled in this example, which could not be the case in a real scenario. The use of the `boolean` constructor is compelling but must be used carefully as the value `false` will result in a `boolean` `true` value. If the value is not controlled and part of a string, the safest way is to compare to use the `isTrue` function provided in this section of the book.

Null

The value `Null` can be assigned to a variable when the main value is not available. Without the compiler option, `strictNullChecks`, TypeScript allows having null or undefined. As a best practice, it's always better to set the strict null check and assign manually which of the variables can have both values. The reason is that you can carefully craft each variable and type with the right amount of flexibility around what is of the specific type or null or undefined, without having a door wide open. Every time a variable can be null, a check to null will be required before being able to use the object's properties:

```
let n1: string | null = Math.random() > 0.5 ? null : "test";
// console.log(n1.substring(0, 1)); // Won't compile since can be null

if (n1 !== null) {
    console.log(n1.substring(0, 1));
}
```

The usage of `null` should be limited in TypeScript in favor of `undefined`. The reason will be explained in the *Undefined* section.

With `strictNullChecks` activated, the `null` value can only be assigned to a type allowing `null` or to a value of type any. To have a type accepting null, a union must be used:

```
let primitiveWithNull: number | null = null;
```

Undefined

The `undefined` can be assigned to a variable when the main value is not available, similar to `null`:

```
let n2: string | undefined = Math.random() > 0.5 ? undefined : "test";
// console.log(n2.substring(0, 1)); // Won't compile since can be null

if (n2 !== null) {
    console.log(n2.substring(0, 1));
}
```

However, it has more cases. For example, an optional parameter (that we will discuss later in this book) is automatically set to `undefined` when not provided by the TypeScript. The reason is that when a property does not exist in JavaScript, it is undefined, not null:

```
function f1(optional?: string): void {
    if (optional === undefined) {
        // Optional parameter was not provided OR was set to undefined
    } else {
        // The optional parameter is for sure a string (not undefined)
    }
}
```

As mentioned, `undefined` is also the value returned if you are using square brackets to access an object property that doesn't exist using a string:

```
let obj = { test: 1 };
console.log(obj["notInObject"]);
```

`undefined` is also the value assigned to a field variable of a class when the class has not yet set the initial value from the constructor. This is only reproducible if the compiler option `strictPropertyInitialization` is set to `false`, which is a bad practice. As a good way to avoid having a field that is not explicitly mentioning `undefined` to be undefined because of a lack of initialization, the compiler option should always be `true`.

With `strictNullChecks` activated, the undefined value can only be assigned to a type allowing `undefined`, a type that is optional, or to a value of type any. To have a type accept `undefined`, a union must be used with the primitive and undefined. In the case of an optional, a function can use the question mark before the colon that specifies the primitive:

```
let primitiveWithUndefined: number | undefined = undefined;

function functOptionalArg(primitiveOptional?: number): void {
    // ...
}

functOptionalArg();
functOptionalArg(undefined);
functOptionalArg(1);
```

An `undefined` can also use the optional notation in a class or an interface as follows:

```
interface InterfaceWithUndefined {
    m1?: number;
}
```

Like a type in a union with `undefined`, an optional value can be verified by comparing against `undefined`:

```
let i1: InterfaceWithUndefined = {};
let i2: InterfaceWithUndefined = { m1: undefined };

console.log(i1.m1 === undefined); // True
console.log(i2.m1 === undefined); // True
```

Symbol

A `Symbol` allows the creation of a value that is unique. A `Symbol` is different than a constant because two constants with the same value are equal, while this is not the case with two symbols with the same value. The constant variables work like any variable, by comparing the value. Comparisons with `Symbol` work differently. Every `Symbol` is unique, hence even with the same value, they are not the same. Let's see some examples:

```
const s2 = Symbol("s");
const c1 = "s";
const c2 = "s";

if(isSymbolEqualS(s2)){
    console.log("Symbols are equal"); // Won't print
```

```
    }
    if(c1 === c2){
        console.log("Constants are equal");
    }

    function isSymbolEqualS(p1:Symbol): boolean{
        return Symbol("s") === p1;
    }
```

The use of `Symbol` can ensure that the value provided is absolutely the one desired. It is not able to pass another constant with the same value, neither a string with the same value. Only the exact same symbol must be used:

```
let s100 = Symbol("same");
let s101 = Symbol("same");

if (s100 === s101) {
 console.log("Same"); // Won't print
}
```

Finally, `Symbol` can be used as an insurance when defining a field to an object. With the symbol, you can be sure to define every field once. A `Symbol` is by nature immutable:

```
const field1 = Symbol("field");
const obj = {
    [field1]: "field1 value"
};

console.log(obj[field1]); // Print "field1 value"
```

TypeScript needs to know about the `Symbol` feature that was introduced in ES2015. Before using the `Symbol` keyword, the `tsconfig.json` must add `lib` to the array:

```
"lib": [
 "es2015",
 "es2015.symbol"
 ]
```

Non-primitive

There is also a more advanced group of variables beyond the primitives. The non-primitive group includes `void`, `string literal`, `tuple`, `any`, `unknown`, and `never`; we will now discuss these variables.

What is void?

A `void` is a special and is used mainly for a function that returns no value. With an explicit return to `void`, the function cannot accept a return statement with a value that can occur with it; hence, it acts as a guard of potential error of returning a value. A `void` function can still have an empty return to leave the function before reaching the closing curly bracket. A `void` variable can only be assigned to `undefined`:

```
let a: void = undefined;
console.log(a);
```

This is not useful, but it explains what happens if you return a function without a value to a `void` function:

```
function returnNothing():void{
    return;
}
console.log(returnNothing()); // undefined
```

It is always a good practice to mark a function with `void` instead of using the implicit return value. The implicit return type for a function is a *weak void* because the function allows the returning of anything. The following function doesn't have a return type and was initially returning nothing. However, in its life, the function changed (as you will see next) and now returns three different values that are not like the previous ones. The *implicit returns* value is not void anymore. Having an explicit return type define a contract and indicate to anyone touching the function what is the expected return type and that should be respected. In this example code, the function returns a union of a Boolean, number, and string:

```
function returnWithoutType(i: number) {
    if (i === 0) {
        return false;
    } else if (i < 0) {
        return -1;
    } else {
        return "positive";
    }
}
```

The reasons to avoid using any type

The `any` is a wildcard type that allows not only `any` type but also to change the type at will. There are many problems with `any`. The first one is that it is hard to follow what type is a variable; we are back to how JavaScript is written:

```
let changeMe: any;
changeMe = 1;
changeMe = "string too";
changeMe = false;
```

The use of `any` should be avoided because it can hold a value that is not as expected and still it can compile because TypeScript does not know the type and cannot perform validation:

```
let anyDangerous: any = false; // still not a boolean, neither a string
console.log(changeMe.subString(0, 1)); // Compile, but crash at runtime
```

The only reason to use `any` is in two situations. The first one is that you are migrating code from JavaScript to TypeScript. Migrating code can take a long time and TypeScript is built naturally in a way that you can be in a hybrid mode for a while. It means that not only you can turn down some strictness of the compiler options, but also that you can create functions, variables, and types that are not fully detailed in terms of type by allowing `any`.

The second situation where `any` is potentially acceptable is when you are in a situation that you cannot figure out the type in some advanced scenario and you must move on. The latter should be a signpost and must have a follow-up because we do not want to make it a habit.

Usage of the never type

The `never` is a variable that should never be set. This might sound useless at first but can be useful in a case where you want to ensure that nothing falls into a particular code path. A function rarely returns `never`, but it can happen. This is the case if you are having a function that does not allow you to finish the method to execute or return any variable; hence, it never fully returns. This can be coded using an exception:

```
function returnNever(i: number): never {
   // Logic here
   
   if (i === 0) {
      throw Error("i is zero");
   } else {
```

```
        throw Error("i is not zero");
    }

    // Will never reach the end of the function
}
```

`Never` occurs when you are writing code and you are writing a condition that cannot occur and that TypeScript infers the type by the usage of your code. This can happen if you have several conditions and that one englobe another making some variable fall into the `never` scenario. It can also happen if you have all the variable values covered by condition and have an `else` statement (or default with a `switch case`). The value cannot have any other value than *never been assigned*, since all values are checked. Here is an illustration of the possibility:

```
type myUnion = "a" | "b";

function elseNever(value: myUnion) {
    if (value === "a") {
        value; // type is "a"
    } else if (value === "b") {
        value; // type is "b"
    } else {
        value; // type is never
    }
}
```

In practice, the `never` type is used for checking whether all values of an `enum` or a `union` have conditions that took care of all the values. This allows creating a validation when a developer adds a value to the `enum` or the `union` but forgets to add a condition. The lack of the condition makes the code fall through the exhaustive check. TypeScript is smart enough to verify all cases and understand that the code might go in the function that takes a `never` parameter, which is not allowed because nothing can be assigned to `never`:

```
type myUnion = "a" | "b";
let c: myUnion = Math.random() > 0.5 ? "a" : "b";

if (c == "a") {
    console.log("Union a");
} else {
    exhaustiveCheck(c); //"b" will fallthrough
}

function exhaustiveCheck(x: never): never {
    throw new Error("");
}
```

Unknown type to have a stricter any type

TypeScript `unknown` type is a new addition to reduce the usage of `any`. When a variable is of type `unknown`, everything can be set to the variable. However, the value `unknown` can only be set to another `unknown` type or `any` type. Here is a list of several rules about the `unknown` type:

- An `unknown` type can only be used with the equality operator; no other operator will compile.
- A function that returns `unknown` does not require to return anything.
- An intersection with the `unknown` type is useless because the type on which the unknown is intersected will take over. However, when used in a `union`, it will always take precedence and override any other type in the union.
- A key of on an `unknown` type is always `never`.

One use case of the type `unknown` is that it can be used when you do not know a type. Instead of relying on `any`, which can accept everything and be passed along any code, the use of `unknown` restricts the flow of the variable. Since an unknown variable cannot be set to another variable, it forces the developer to properly scope down the value to its type and continue further along. Without the `unknown` type, `any` would have been the only option. It opens the door wide to accept anything and to:

```
function f1(x: any): string {
  return x;
}

function f2(x: unknown): string {
  return x; // Does not compile
}
```

In this example, the first function can take anything and expect to return a string. However, no cast or anything is required because a variable of type `any` can return a string. However, with an `unknown`, it must be handled. As mentioned, the reason is that the `unknown` type cannot be assigned to types other than `unknown` or `any`.

Enforcing a type in a list

An array can be created in two different ways. The first is using the square brackets and by using the `Array` generic object. They are both interchangeable, and both of them can be typed.

The square-bracket format is more compact, and it allows to specify the type before the squared brackets. The `Array` generic object specifies the type between the smaller/bigger sign:

```
let arrayWithSquareBrackets: number[] = [1, 2, 3];
let arrayWithObject: Array<number> = [1, 2, 3];
let arrayWithObjectNew: Array<number> = new Array<number>(1, 2 ,3);
```

It is possible to have an array holding more than one type of a type by combining the array type with a union:

```
let arrayWithSquareBrackets2: (number | string)[] = [1, 2, "one", "two"];
let arrayWithObject2: Array<number | string> = [1, 2, "one", "two"];
```

TypeScript acts the same as in JavaScript, other than specifying the type for the array. You can access the content by using the index position and using all the methods available that are automatically typed with the type of the type specified for the array:

```
const position1 = arrayWithObject2[0]; // 1
const unexisting = arrayWithObject2[100]; // undefined
```

If a position doesn't contain a value, the type returned is undefined.

TypeScript allows to loop an array and retrieve for each position the element strongly typed. The type is optional because TypeScript can infer the type. It means that the following code can be written with or without the `number` type:

```
arrayWithSquareBrackets.forEach(function (element: number){
  console.log(element);
});
```

Defining a conscribed set of constants with enum

TypeScript has a keyword `enum` that let you specify many possible values as a group where only a single item can be selected. Defining an `enum` can be done by providing potential keys that would automatically assign a sequential number from 0 to the first potential choice of the `enum` and so on:

```
enum Weather {
    Sunny,
    Cloudy,
    Rainy,
    Snowy
}
```

It is possible to specify a value to a key to have fine-grained control. Any missing value will be the next sequence value. In the following code example, `Sunny` is set to `100`, and `Cloudy` is automatically `101`, `Rainy` is `102`, and so on:

```
enum Weather {
    Sunny = 100,
    Cloudy,
    Rainy,
    Snowy
}
```

It is possible to skip, in that case, you can only provide a bigger value and the value of the assigned one is sequential. In the following code example, the values are `100`, `101`, `200`, and `201`:

```
enum Weather {
    Sunny = 100,
    Cloudy,
    Rainy = 200,
    Snowy
}
```

The `enum` can also support string or a mix of a string and a number:

```
enum Weather {
    Sunny = "Sun",
    Cloudy = "Cloud",
    Rainy = 200,
    Snowy
}
```

The `enum` can be accessed by the `enum` or by value. Accessing by the `enum` requires using the dot notation from the `enum` directly. The value returned is the `enum`. This is the common way to assign an `enum` in TypeScript. It is also possible to assign the value. The assignation by value is useful when data come from JSON. For example, the value is returned from an Ajax response. It bridges non-TypeScript into TypeScript:

```
let today: Weather = Weather.Cloudy;
let tomorrow: Weather = 200;

console.log("Today value", today); // Today value Cloud
console.log("Today key", Weather[today]); // Today key undefined
console.log("Tommorow value", tomorrow); // Tommorow value 200
console.log("Tommorow key", Weather[tomorrow]); // Tommorow key Rainy
```

In the previous code, accessing the value from the with the square bracket only works when the value in the square bracket is the type, not the value.

In addition to `number` and `string`, `enum` supports bitwise values with the help of a bit shift operator. It allows to check whether a value contains a single or an aggregate of value with an ampersand (`&`). The reason is that with the pipe `|` you can create a variable that contains several values. The stacking values can also reside inside the `enum` for reusability purposes but is not required:

```
enum Weather {
   Sunny = 0,
   Cloudy = 1 << 0,
   Rainy = 1 << 1,
   Snowy = 1 << 2,
   Stormy = Cloudy | Rainy // Can reside inside
}

let today: Weather= Weather.Snowy | Weather.Cloudy; // Can be outside as well

if (today & Weather.Rainy) { // Check
    console.log("Bring an umbrella");
}
```

A value can hold more than a single value. This is useful if we want to persist the existing value intact and you need to use the sign `|=`. To remove a particular status, you need to use `&= ~`. Using these operators will swap the value at the right position in its binary format without affecting the remaining parts of the number:

```
today |= Weather.Rainy;
today &= ~Weather.Snowy;
console.log(today); // 3 -> 011 = Cloudy and Rainy
```

Finally, to check whether the variable is of a particular status, you must use the triple equals with the ampersand to the value you want to check against. The use of a single ampersand for comparison is a mistake. The ampersand returns a number, not a `boolean`. The comparison needs to be against the value that we want to check. It is possible to check against many values by creating a combined value in the comparison:

```
if (Weather.Rainy === (today & Weather.Rainy)) { // Check
  console.log("Rainy");
}

if (Weather.Cloudy === (today & Weather.Cloudy)) { // Check
  console.log("Cloudy");
```

```
}
if ((Weather.Cloudy & Weather.Rainy) === (today & Weather.Cloudy &
Weather.Rainy)) { // Check
  console.log("Cloudy and Rainy");
}
```

The `enum` is a great way to define a set of potential value from a specific domain for a variable. It has the convenience of being clear by naming the choices at your convenience and letting you decide the value of each entry if needed.

String literal and its difference compared to a string

A `string` is a type that allows any kind of characters. A `string literal` is the association of a particular `string` as a type. When a `string` is set to a type, it is possible to assign one value and change it later. The only value possible to set to a `string literal` is the exact string stamped at the declaration:

```
let x: string = "Value1";
x = "Value2";

let y: "Literal";
y = "Literal";
y = "sdasd"; // Won't compile
```

TypeScript compiles the code into plain JavaScript, without types. A `string literal` ensures that while writing the code in TypeScript that only a single string value can be associated with a variable, and this is compiled into JavaScript objects with this mandatory value. The essence of this particularity is that we have in both languages the assurance that the value is unique. This becomes handy in a situation where you need to condition a type that will not be there once compiled. For example, the case of an interface and a piece of code that must act differently depending on the interface. Having a shared field (with the name) among the interfaces with a unique string literal allow comparison at design time and run-time. At design time, TypeScript will be able to narrow down the type and hence provide better support for the specified type and at run-time be able to conduct the execution flow at the right place:

```
interface Book {
    type: "book";
    isbn: string;
    page: number;
}

interface Movie {
```

```
    type: "movie";
    lengthMinutes: number;
}

let hobby: Movie = { type: "movie", lengthMinutes: 120 };

function showHobby(hobby: Book | Movie): void {
    if (hobby.type === "movie") {
        console.log("Long movie of " + hobby.lengthMinutes);
    } else {
        console.log("A book of few pages: " + hobby.page);
    }
}
```

The code example shows that two interfaces share a type that is a `string literal`. To be able to access the unique property of one or the other `interface` in the function, a comparison of a discriminator is required. Without the comparison, the function that takes both interfaces with the union as a parameter does not know which of the two types is passed. However, TypeScript analyzes the two interfaces and identifies a common field and allows you to use this before scoping down the type. Once TypeScript can find which type is treated, it allows using the specific field of the type. In the example, inside the condition, all the movie's `interface` fields are available. On the other side, the `else` allows all the book's `interface` fields only.

A literal string is one type of three possible literals that TypeScript supports. TypeScript supports `number` and `boolean` on top of the string. Finally, when using `string literal`, always provide the type using the colon:

```
let myLiteral: "onlyAcceptedValue" = "onlyAcceptedValue";
```

Instead of relying on `let`, which opens the door to many assignations, the use of `const` can ensure a single assignation; hence, it will automatically infer a `literal` type for the three types:

```
const myLiteral = "onlyAcceptedValue"; // Not a string
```

It is possible to create a literal by omitting the type only if declared with `const` because the value cannot change; hence, TypeScript will scope to its most narrowed expression. However, a change from `const` to `let` in the future would change the type back to `string`. I suggest being as explicit as possible to avoid an undesired type of change.

Crafting a typed function

Functions are first-class citizens in JavaScript. Since the early versions of ECMAScript, functions were the main concept to execute code and create scope. TypeScript uses the function the same way but provides additional typing features.

A function has a main signature that contains the name of this one, the list of parameters, and the return type. Parameters are defined in parentheses, as in JavaScript, but each parameter will be followed by its type using the colon syntax:

```
function funct1(param1: number): string { return ""; }
```

A `function` can have several parameters of a different type:

```
function funct2(param1: boolean, param2: string): void { }
```

It can also have a parameter that has more than one type using a union:

```
function funct3(param1: boolean | string): void { }
```

A `function` has a single return declaration but that type can use a union to allow types:

```
function funct4(): string | number | boolean { return ""; }
```

A function can have a complimentary signature to indicate to the consumer which parameters match together and with the return type. Having several function signatures for the same body is the concept of an overloaded function. When using an overloaded function, all signatures must be written from top to bottom from the most specific to the largest one. All the definition requires finishing with a semicolon expect the last one. The last signature always has a union that covers all possible types for each position. In the following code example, we specify that if the parameter is a `boolean`, then the function returns a string. If the parameter is a `Date`, then the return type is a `number`. The last signature contains a first parameter the union of both possible values (`boolean` and date) as well as a union for the return type between `string` and `number`):

```
function funct5(param1: boolean): string;
function funct5(param1: Date): number;
function funct5(param1: boolean | Date): string | number {
    if (typeof param1 === "boolean") {
        return param1 ? "Yes" : "No";
    } else {
        return 0;
    }
}
```

```
}
const expectedString: string = funct5(true); // Yes
const expectedNumber: number = funct5(new Date()); // 0
```

A function can be anonymous. Here is an example with the *fat arrow* format and one example returning a `Function` constructor:

```
function returnAnAnonymousFunction(): () => number {
    return () => 1;
}

function returnAnAnonymousFunction2(): Function {
    return function () { return 1 };
}
```

A `function` can be a `variable` function or a typical function. Here are three functions set in a `variable`. The `variable` can be called by using parentheses and the required parameter. The code example shows also two ways to return data with the *fat arrow* format. If the code returns directly without doing any *several* statements, the need for curly brackets and *return statement* is not needed:

```
const variable = (message: string) => message + " world";
const variable2 = (message: string) => { return message + " world" };
const variable3 = function (message: string) { return message + " world" };

variable("Hello");
```

A function can have an optional parameter and a default value parameter. An optional parameter is denoted by the use of question mark after the name of the parameter. An optional parameter allows avoiding passing a value. `TypeScript` automatically sets the parameter to `undefined`:

```
function functWithOptional(param1?: boolean): void { }
functWithOptional();
functWithOptional(undefined);
functWithOptional(true);
```

`Optional` is different than having the variable with a union to `undefined` because the union requires passing the value or undefined while optional allows passing the value, undefined or nothing:

```
function functWithUndefined(param1: boolean | undefined): void { }
functWithUndefined(true);
functWithUndefined(undefined);
```

`Optional` can only be set after non-optional parameter. The reason is that other parameters are required but having `Optional` before or in the middle would make it hard to map which parameter is which. The following code example presents a case where the function does not compile because of that rule. However, it's possible to have many optional parameters:

```
function functWithOptional2(param1?: boolean, param2: string): void { } // Doesn't compile
function functWithOptional3(param1?: boolean, param2?: string): void { }
```

A `function` can be in a class (object-oriented is covered in a future chapter). When this happens, the syntax is different. It doesn't use the keyword `function`. Instead, the visibility is provided, which is `public`, `private`, or `protected`. `TypeScript` allows avoiding access modifiers, which will result in a `public` function. As for a class variable, the omission of the visibility uses `public` as default:

```
class ClassFullOfFunctions {
    public f1() { }
    private f2(p1: number): string { return ""; }
    protected f3(): void { }
    f4(): boolean { return true; }
    f5(): void { } // Public
}
```

The basis remains the same with parameters and a return type that is strongly typed. It is also possible to create a variable that holds the function inside a class as seen in this chapter. Here are three examples of a `private` function defined as a `variable`. The first one is long and very explicit. The second example doesn't define the type at the function level because it is already defined in the declaration. The last example doesn't define the type of the variable and the variable is still strongly typed because it infers its signature from the initialization:

```
private long: (p1: number) => string = (p1: number) => { return ""; }
private short: (p1: number) => string = (p1) => "";
private tiny = (p1: number) => "";
```

A `function` in a variable is technically called a **function expression**, while the more traditional `function` syntax is named a **function statement**. The usage of one or the other is the same in `TypeScript` than with `JavaScript`. Because it operates under JavaScript's law, it means that the expression function is not hoisted.

How to be strongly typed without specifying the type

TypeScript can have a type specified explicitly or you can have the type determined by TypeScript. The latter is called an **implicit type** or a type defined by inference. The action of inference is conducted by TypeScript depending on how a variable is initialized during declaration for the variable or what is returned for a function return type.

A variable inference is only possible when a value is assigned at the declaration. It means that you must set a value when using `var/let/const`:

```
const x = 1;
let y = 1;
let z;
// ...
z = 1;
```

In the previous code example, the value 1 is assigned to the variables x and y during the initialization. This is valid even if the colon is not used. `TypeScript` will infer the type for both variables. In the case of not specifying a value, only `var` or `let` would compile because it allows in a future moment the assignment. The value is not specified, which means that the type is falling back to `any`. This is true even if the value is set within the scope of the variable life.

In the previous code example, the value 1 was assigned to a constant and a variable. The type of both of these declarators is different. The constant type is not a number, it is a number literal of 1. It means that the type is 1 and only 1 and not any other number. However, the type of the variable declared with `let` is `number`. The reason is that with the constant, TypeScript knows that it can only be initialized once and that the value cannot change. It scopes down the simplest type it can find which is the value of the primitive. On the contrary, the variable declared with `let` can change its value during the lifetime of the variable. The TypeScript scopes the type every number. This is `true` with a `number`, `string`, and `boolean`:

```
const d1 = new Date();
let d2 = new Date();

const b1 = true;
let b2 = false;

const c1 = {
 m1: 1
};
```

[51]

Onboarding Types with Primitive

```
let c2 = {
  m1: 1
};
```

However, a date will stay to the date type regardless of the declarator, the same for any class or interface because it is the smaller denominator. In the previous code example, both `c1` and `c2` are of the type of an object that must have a member named `m1` of a type number. This example illustrates how TypeScript can also infer type inside type. `m1` is a number by inference.

Inference works with functions as well. However, it has some limitations. The first one is that parameter must be explicit. The reason is that you cannot infer by usage without having a potential room for error. In the following code, the argument `a` is implicit `any`:

```
function f1(a) {
    return a;
}
```

However, the return can be implicit. By returning a known type, the return type can be defined:

```
function f2(a: number) {
    return a;
}
```

In the case of returning several values, TypeScript creates a union of all potential types. In the following code example, there are two return statements. TypeScript looks for each value returned and concludes that two different values are returned. The return type generated is `number | string`:

```
function f3() {
    if (true) {
        return 1;
    } else {
        return "1";
    }
}
```

Summary

In this chapter, we saw how TypeScript can declare variables and which declarator is be the best to use depending on the situation. We saw that TypeScript improves JavaScript's primitive type by enforcing the type during the lifetime of the variable. We explained how to transform a variable into a multiple type container with the concept of the union. TypeScript brings type to functions and we saw how we could improve the readability of a function that takes many combinations of arguments and return types with the overload function. TypeScript brings a new way to type variables with the popular `enum` borrowed from popular languages such as Java and C#. Finally, we glimpsed at how TypeScript is smart to infer types in different situations that can be advantageous to reduce lengthy definitions.

In the next chapter, we will see in detail the differences between many different object types and look at how we can manipulate types to have a strongly typed code flexible enough to fulfil our needs of defining our business models with TypeScript.

3
Unleashing the Power of Type with Objects

TypeScript can be overwhelming with all the different objects. In this chapter, we illustrate the difference between an `object`, `Object`, `object literal`, and an object built with a constructor. This chapter also discusses the notion of a union between types that will allow an infinite combination of types for a single value. Furthermore, the concept of an intersection looms, giving the possibility of manipulating type differently. At the end of this chapter, the reader will be able to create complex combinations of objects that hold advanced structures. We will dissect how to create a dictionary with a strongly typed index signature, understand how type can be beneficial with a map, and learn how to use the right object to be as accurate as possible when defining an object that can have a broad reach.

This chapter covers the following topics:

- How to strongly type a set/dictionary with an index signature
- TypeScript and map
- The difference between an index signature and a map
- The difference between `object` and `Object`
- When to use `object`, `Object`, or any
- What is an `object literal`
- How to create a 'constructed object
- The difference between an explicit type or a cast
- Variable with many types
- Combining a type with an intersection
- Intersecting with something other than a type
- Intersecting with an optional type
- Merging a type with inheritance
- The difference between a type and an interface

- Destructuring a type and an array
- Tuple
- The difference between declare and `let/const/var`

How to strongly type a set/dictionary with an index signature

Besides an array, a *set* or a *dictionary* is a common structure to store unstructured data for quick access. In JavaScript, using the dynamic notion of being able to assign a member to an object creates a dictionary. Each object's property becomes a key of the dictionary. TypeScript's types above this pattern with *index signature*. It allows you to specify the type of the key (between number and string) and any type of values:

```
interface Person {
  [id: string]: string;
}
```

Writing into the dictionary is as simple as using the square bracket and assigning the value that must respect the right side of the definition. In the following code example, the key and the value are strings:

```
const p: Person = {};

p["id-1"] = "Name1";
p["string-2"] = "Name12";

console.log(p["string-2"]); // Name12
```

An index signature can be tricky because of historical reasons. For example, if the index is defined to accept a string as the key, you will be able to pass a string and a number as well. The other way around is not true: a key with a number type does not accept a string:

```
const c: Person = {
  "test": "compile",
  123: "compile too" // Key is number even if Person requires string: it compiles
};

interface NotAPerson {
  [id: number]: string;
}
```

```
// DOES NOT COMPILE:
const c2: NotAPerson = {
  "test": "compile", // THIS LINE DOES NOT COMPILE
  123: "compile too"
};
```

The last example illustrates more than a single issue with the type of key. The code uses a syntax to define a value for an index signature directly by using an `object literal` where all members are the keys and their value the index signature's value. This is the syntax to use to initialize default value, while the other way, with square brackets, is the way to add dynamically and access value rapidly.

Additionally, TypeScript allows you to access a member of an object with a square bracket by providing the name of the member as a string. The distinction with index signature is that TypeScript won't let you read or add a member if the index signature is not provided in your definition:

```
interface NotIndexSignatureObject {
    name: string;
    count: number;
}

const obj: NotIndexSignatureObject = {
    name: "My Name",
    count: 123
};

console.log(obj["doesNotExist"]); // Does not compile
console.log(obj["name"]); // Compile
```

Another quirk with index signature is when it is combined with an object that has other members. The key of the index signature can be only of a string with members returning a string. It means that most of the time you will have to fall back with a key of a number. The following code does not compile:

```
interface ObjWithMembersAndIndexSignature {
    name: string;
    count: number;
    when: Date;
    [id: string]: string; // DOES NOT COMPILE
}
```

By contrast, the following code compiles but is fragile. The reason it compiles is that in some very rare cases, TypeScript automatically converts types back to a string, depending on its usage. In that case, the `number` and `Date` of the member `count` and `when` is accepted to be a string. However, a tiny change of adding a member that has an object will disrupt that rule. The two following blocks of code illustrate that change. This following block contains a primitive:

```
interface ObjWithMembersAndIndexSignature {
  name: string;
  count: number;
  when: Date;
  [id: number]: string; // COMPILE
}
```

This second block contains an additional object that is not allowed when an index signature is defined:

```
interface ObjWithMembersAndIndexSignature2 {
  name: string;
  count: number;
  when: Date;
  obj: { s: string }; // DOES NOT COMPILE
  [id: number]: string | number | Date;
}
```

Another compilation issue you might have is to add a string key to an object with an index signature that has a key to a number:

```
const obj2: ObjWithMembersAndIndexSignature = {
    name: "My Name",
    count: 123,
    when: new Date(),
    "more": "nooo" // DOES NOT COMPILE
};
```

You can transform the object definition by providing a member of a type number with a value of a string:

```
 const obj3: ObjWithMembersAndIndexSignature = {
   name: "My Name",
   count: 123,
   when: new Date(),
   12: "string only" // Good if number->string
};
```

However, if you want to have a string as a key you will need to change the type allowed as a value in your index signature to have a union of every member:

```
interface ObjWithMembersAndIndexSignature2 {
    name: string;
    count: number;
    when: Date;
    [id: string]: string | number | Date;
}
```

To conclude with index signature, it is wise to have your mapping object small and without too many members, to allow having an index signature that can be accessed without requiring to narrow the type. For example, the last code example was returning a string or a number or a date. This means that every access to the object is required to check the type before consuming its properties. However, having an interface that has only the index signature can be used as a property of an object and have all the quick access without needing to narrow down. Here is the code that illustrates the pattern:

```
interface MyMap<T> {
    [index: string]: T;
}

interface YourBusinessLogicObject {
    oneProps: string;
    secondProps: number;
    thirdProps: Date;
    yourDictionary: MyMap<string>;
}
```

TypeScript and map

We discussed creating a dictionary/set with the index signature that leverages the flexibility of an object. An alternative is the use of a `map` class. A `map` is a class that can be instantiated with or without values, and it is a type of object that is not unique to TypeScript. ECMAScript defines how a map is structured and behaves; TypeScript is providing a type on top of the class.

A map has the same capability of fast access than index signature. The following code instantiates the `Map` with two key-values entries. The key and the value can be anything. What is important in the constructor is when providing a value, this one must be iterable:

```
let map = new Map([["key1", "value1"], ["key2", "value2"]]);

let value1: string | undefined = map.get("key1");
```

The previous code not only created a map but also accessed a value by using a key of the same type as defined in the constructor. If a key does not exist in the map, an undefined value is returned, similar to the index signature. The next code example creates two maps, without providing initial values. The first one doesn't use the generic definition; hence, falls back to the type `any` for the key and the value. However, the second line shows an initialization that specifies the generic type to have a key of string and a value of a number. Even if the map does not have values specified at the initialization, the latter still provides a strongly typed enforcement for a future value set by the function set:

```
let map2 = new Map(); // Key any, value any
let map3 = new Map<string, number>(); // Key string, value number
```

The following code does not compile because the key type must be the same. In the code example, it has a number and a string:

```
let map4 = new Map([[1, "value1"], ["key2", "value2"]]); // Doesn't compile
```

A map has many functions other than get. It can *set* values, which is handy when you do not have all the values of the creation of the map. A map can also look up to see whether a key exists in the map by returning `true` or `false`. Finally, it is possible to remove an entry with a function instead of relying on the `delete` keyword for an index signature:

```
map.set("key3", "value3");
map.has("key1");
map.delete("key1"); // Similar to delete obj.key1 (index signature)
```

The differences between index signature and a map

The differences between using a map or an index signature pattern with an object are slim. Here are two lists of the pros of each structure:

Object:

- Can have more than just a key-value. It can have functions and other members.
- An object coming from JSON is automatically compatible with an index signature, while a map would require a manual mapping.
- An object pattern is faster at accessing data than the map, and uses less memory for a small set of data and a medium set of data. This is true with Chrome, but benchmarks are not consistent among browsers, as well as the overall size of the map/object.

Map:

- A map performs better when many add and delete. It uses a hashing function underneath.
- It preserves the order when an element is added. This might be an advantage, since a map is naturally iterable.
- A map performs better with a large set of data.
- A map's key is not limited to a number or a string for a key.

The differences between object and Object

There are many object types in TypeScript. There is `Object`, `object`, `class object`, and `object literal`. In this section, we will cover the differences between an `Object` (uppercase) and an `object` (lowercase).

The `Object` type that starts with a capital letter, or the uppercase one, or with the big O represents something ubiquitous, a cross type that is available with every type and object. The capital letter Object carries a common set of functions. Here is the list of its available functions:

```
toString(): string;
toLocaleString(): string;
valueOf(): Object;
hasOwnProperty(v: string): boolean;
isPrototypeOf(v: Object): boolean;
propertyIsEnumerable(v: string): boolean;
```

A huge set of types comes under the umbrella of `Object`. Assigning several different values to an object of type `Object` shows the flexibility of the type and how broad the potential range of types is:

```
let bigObject: Object;
bigObject = 1;
bigObject = "1";
bigObject = true;
bigObject = Symbol("123");
bigObject = { a: "test" };
bigObject = () => { };
bigObject = [1, 2, 3];
bigObject = new Date();
bigObject = new MyClass();
bigObject = Object.create({});
```

The lowercase object coverts everything that is not a number, a string, a `boolean`, a `null`, an `undefined`, or a `Symbol`. The lowercase `object` is a subset of the uppercase `Object`. It contains `object literals`, dates, functions, arrays, and an instance of an object created with `new` and `create`:

```
let littleObject: object;

littleObject = { a: "test" };
littleObject = new Date();
littleObject = () => { };
littleObject = [1, 2, 3];
littleObject = new MyClass();
littleObject = Object.create({});
```

In the cases of `null` and `undefined`, they are neither `object` nor `Object`. They are in a special category and are a subtype of all other types. TypeScript's compiler must be configured with the strict option `"strictNullCheck"`, which is the de-factor configuration value, meaning that even if `null` and `undefined` are a subset of all types, only a union of the main type and `null` or `undefined` will allow the assignment to either of these two special values:

```
let acceptNull: number | null = null;
acceptNull = 1;

let acceptUndefined: number | undefined = 1;
acceptUndefined = null;
```

When to use object, Object, or any

Which type of object to use is a sub-question of the previous one that was discussing the differences between `object`, `Object`, and `any`. The rule of thumb is to always use the more conscribe type. It means to avoid using both `object` and `Object` as much as possible. However, in a case where you need to cover a wider range of types and you cannot define them with a union, the use of `object` is better if you do not need a primitive, because it has less potential values.

Both `object` and `Object` are better than `any` because `any` allows accessing any members of any type while `object` will limit you to the following:

```
let obj1: Object = {};
let obj2: object = {};
let obj3: {} = {};
let obj4: any = {};
```

```
obj1.test = "2"; // Does not compile
obj2.test = "2"; // Does not compile
obj3.test = "2"; // Does not compile
obj4.test = "2";

obj1.toString();
obj2.toString();
obj3.toString();
obj4.toString();
```

If you do not know the type and need to take an object, you should use an `object` (lowercase) if you are not allowing a primitive. You should fallback to `Object` (uppercase) if you support a primitive and in the last resort use `any`. However, a better potential approach is, if possible, to use a generic type that allows avoiding doing a type check and casting, which is often a pitfall of using something such as `object` and `Object`.

What is an object literal?

An `object literal` is an `object` created with curly brackets. An `object literal` is an `Object` and an `object`. You can define the type for an `object literal` with `type` or `interface`. It is a quick way to have data in a structure that is typed. The `object literal` inherits from `Object` (uppercase).

```
type ObjLiteralType = { x: number, y: number };
interface ObjLiteralType2 {
  x: number;
  y: number;
}
```

We can do a quick test with four functions and see that the `object literal` is accepted in all of the functions, even if the parameter's type is different among all the function's signature:

```
function uppercaseObject(obj: Object): void { }
function lowercaseObject(obj: object): void { }
function anyObject(obj: any): void { }
function objectLiteral(obj: {}): void { }

uppercaseObject({ x: 1 });
lowercaseObject({ x: 1 });
anyObject({ x: 1 });
objectLiteral({ x: 1 });
```

Two (or more) objects that literally have the same structure are interchangeable. You can define an object literal and set it in a variable that defines the same structure in the interface. You can also do the same if the type is anonymous or inferred. Here are the four ways to create a typed `object literal`. They are all assignable to one another because they share the same structure. This is a strength of TypeScript, as it is a structural language, as opposed to a nominal language:

```
let literalObject: ObjLiteralType = { x: 1, y: 2 };
let literalObject2: ObjLiteralType2 = { x: 1, y: 2 };
let literalObject3: { x: number, y: number } = { x: 1, y: 2 };
let literalObject4 = { x: 1, y: 2 };

literalObject = literalObject2 = literalObject3 = literalObject4;
```

How to create a constructed object

Finally, a class object is an object defined with the keyword `class` and instantiated with the keyword `new`. Every class can be instantiated more than once. Every instantiation starts with the use of `new`, and every value set in an object remains in that object, with the exception of static fields, which are shared across every instance of the same class. We will see many features of object-oriented and object in a later chapter:

```
class ClassWithConstructor {
    constructor(){
        console.log("Object instantiated");
    }
}
const cwc = new ClassWithConstructor();
```

The creation of the class calls the constructor. In the previous code example, the `console.log` will be called during the instantiation of the class into an object.

The differences between an explicit type and a cast

If you have an interface that you want to build, you can set the variable type with the colon and specify the fields. If a field misses TypeScript will not compile; if there is more than the definition, TypeScript won't compile:

```
interface MyObject {
    a: number;
```

```
    b: string;
}
const newObject1: MyObject = { a: 1, b: "2" };
```

Another way is to avoid specifying the type after the colon and use `as` to cast:

```
const newObject2 = { a: 1, b: "2" } as MyObject;
```

The issue is that cast coerces TypeScript to believe the object is the type specified even if it does not respect the contract. Casting should never be used to define a variable. The reason is that even if the contract is respected initially, if the object changes, the cast will still force the type assignation, but the object will not with the right structure. The following two lines compile but are invalid in term of logic. The first one has an additional member that is not in the interface, and the second line is missing one field:

```
const newObject3 = { a: 1, b: "2", c: "OH NO" } as MyObject;
const newObject4 = { a: 1 } as MyObject;
```

Variable with many types

In many situations, a variable requires having more than one field. For example, you can have a field that only takes a value among a few strings:

```
type MyType = "a" | "b" | "c";
const m1: MyType = "a";
const m2: MyType = "no"; // Doesn't compile
```

The creation of a type with the keyword `type` is not required but allows reusability of the type. The first example was creating a type with many allowed strings. A variable declared with the new type will only accept the strings from the list. However, most of the time, unions are using a more complex type, such as between the interface, type and primitive:

```
type AcceptedOption = number | string | { option1: string, option2: number };
const myOption1: AcceptedOption = "run";
const myOption2: AcceptedOption = 123;
const myOption3: AcceptedOption = { option1: "run", option2: 123 };
```

A function can take a union type as a parameter and return a return type as well. A union is often used to accept a type as well as `undefined`:

```
function functWithUnion(p: boolean | undefined): undefined | null{
    return undefined;
}
```

When using a union, only the common fields are accessible. In the following code, `TypeA` has two fields, `a` and `b`, and `TypeB` has `b` and `c`. The only common field is `b`, which means that it is the only available and accessible field in the function. This is true until we narrow down the type to one of a type in the union. We will see how type narrowing works later:

```
interface TypeA {
    a: string;
    b: string;
}

interface TypeB {
    b: string;
    c: string;
}

function functionWithUnion(param1: TypeA | TypeB): void {
    console.log(param1.b);
}
```

Combining type with intersect

The more you build types, the more you will need a feature to work with them. The intersect feature is one tool in TypeScript's toolbox that lets you merge types together. The intersection symbol is the ampersand (`&`). The following code example shows that we are creating a third type with the combination of two interfaces. The common fields become one, and the difference adds up:

```
interface TypeA {
    a: string;
    b: string;
}
interface TypeB {
    b: string;
    c: string;
}

type TypeC = TypeA & TypeB;
const m: TypeC = {
    a: "A",
    b: "B",
    c: "C",
};
```

Chapter 3

It is possible to intersect generic and primitive as well. The latter is less used, since it is almost not pragmatic. However, the former (generic) is helpful to merge a custom type into a defined contract:

```
interface TypeA {
    a: string;
    b: string;
}
function intersectGeneric<TT1>(t1: TT1): TT1 & TypeA {
    const x: TypeA = { a: "a", b: "b" };
    return (<any>Object).assign({}, x, t1);
}

const result = intersectGeneric({ c: "c" });
console.log(result); // { a: 'a', b: 'b', c: 'c' }
```

The order of the types in the intersection does not matter. Two types created here are exactly the same:

```
type TypeD1 = TypeA & TypeB;
type TypeD2 = TypeB & TypeA;
```

However, even if they are the same, with the same value, each initialization creates a unique object, meaning that comparing them will be false. Regarding comparing two identical types with different names, they are both of type `Object` and the reason is that `typeOf` is a JavaScript operator and the type is removed at run-time; hence, it behaves the same way at design time. To compare type we need a discriminator that we will discuss later:

```
let d1: TypeD1 = { a: "a", b: "b", c: "c" };
let d2: TypeD2 = { a: "a", b: "b", c: "c" };

console.log(typeof d1); // Object
console.log(typeof d2); // Object
console.log(d1 === d2); // False

d2 = d1;
console.log(d1 === d2); // True
```

The use of parentheses does not affect the declaration of the type. The following code is redundant, with the union being useless. Here are four different types that take the same value:

```
type TypeD3 = (TypeA & TypeB) | (TypeB & TypeA);
type TypeD4 = TypeA & TypeB | TypeB & TypeA;
type TypeD5 = (TypeA & TypeB);
```

```
type TypeD6 = TypeA & TypeB;

let d3: TypeD3 = { a: "a", b: "b", c: "c" };
let d4: TypeD4 = { a: "a", b: "b", c: "c" };
let d5: TypeD5 = { a: "a", b: "b", c: "c" };
let d6: TypeD6 = { a: "a", b: "b", c: "c" };
```

Intersecting with something other than a type

It is possible to intersect with a type, primitive, and an interface. Intersecting with primitive is useless, since a number cannot be a boolean at the same time. However, intersecting an interface is valid as much as intersecting with a type. The same rules apply for a type or an interface, with regard to intersecting:

```
interface InterfaceA {
 m1: string;
}

interface InterfaceB {
 m2: string;
}

type TypeAB = InterfaceA & InterfaceB;
```

While the most common case of intersection touches type and interface, it is possible to intersect classes. Intersection with classes are rare and it creates a type that cannot be instantiated. Only the public fields are extracted from each class to create a field:

```
type ClassAb = ClassA & ClassB;
const classAb: ClassAb = { m1: "test", m2: "test2" };
```

Intersecting with an optional type

It is possible to intersect two types with cross properties that have different rules. A field in one type with the mention of an option member can be merged with a type that is not optional. The result is that the field becomes non-optional:

```
interface InterfaceSameField1 {
    m1: string;
}
```

```
interface InterfaceSameField2 {
   m1?: string;
}

type Same = InterfaceSameField1 & InterfaceSameField2;
let same: Same = { m1: "This is required" };
```

The previous code example shows the intersection and the field `m1` being required. If omitted or set to undefined, the code does not compile.

Merge type with inheritance

It is possible to merge two types if these ones are an interface or a class, by using `extends`. Extending an interface with another is an alternative to using the ampersand. In the following code example, the merged interface contains its own member, as well as the member of `InterfaceA` and `InterfaceB`:

```
interface InterfaceA {
  m1: string;
}

interface InterfaceB {
  m2: string;
}

interface InterfaceMergeAB extends InterfaceA, InterfaceB {
  m3: string;
}
```

The differences between type and interface

Type and interface are not exactly the same. For example, you can merge two interfaces together, but you cannot merge an interface with a primitive, which can be done with a type. You can define an interface in many definitions allowed future extension outside the main module. The possibility to enhance an interface in many areas allow many plugins or contract versioning patterns to happen. The technical jargon for this feature is **open-ended**:

```
interface IA {
  m1: string;
}

interface IA {
```

```
    m2: string;
}

const ia: IA = { m1: "m1", m2: "m2" };
```

A class can extend a type or an interface. The latter is often more seen because type carries some caveat. For example, a type that contains a primitive won't be a sound choice for a class because the implementation will not work. TypeScript is smart enough to analyze the content of the type and figure out that the implementation cannot occur:

```
type TPrimitive1 = string;
type TPrimitive2 = { m1: string };

class ExtendPrimitiv1 implements TPrimitive1 { // Does not compile
}

class ExtendPrimitiv2 implements TPrimitive2 { // Compile
 public m1: string = "Compile";
}
```

Type and interface can have an index signature:

```
type TypeWithIndex = {
   [key: string]: string;
   m1: string;
}

const c: TypeWithIndex = {
   m1: "m1"
};

c["m2"] = "m2";
```

The rule of thumb is to rely on an interface as much as possible because of the open-ended feature, the reduction of confusion regarding whether the type can have primitive, and because they can be extended or intersected. The `type` keyword is used to create a union of primitive or to intersect object literals on the fly.

Destructuring a type and an array

Destructuring is a feature of JavaScript that is supported by TypeScript with type protection. Destructuring breaks an object into different pieces. TypeScript brings the type to these pieces.

A scenario is that you need to extract members from an object into a variable. This can be done without destructuring, but it takes several lines of code:

```
interface MyObject {
   id: number;
   time: number;
   name: string;
   startTime: Date;
   stopTime: Date;
   category: string;
}

const obj: MyObject = {
   id: 1,
   time: 100,
   name: "MyName",
   startTime: new Date(),
   stopTime: new Date(),
   category: "Cat5"
};

const id = obj.id;
const name = obj.name;
const category = obj.category;
```

With destructuring, it can be done in a single line. All the variables are from the type of the object. It means that `id` is a new variable of type number, `name` is of the type string, as well as `category`:

```
const { id, name, category } = obj;
```

Destructuring can use the rest operator to take the remainder of the properties not specified. The rest of the syntax is the three dots before the name of the variable that will hold the rest of the members:

```
const { id, name, category, ...remainingMembers } = obj;

remainingMembers.startTime;
remainingMembers.stopTime;
remainingMembers.time;
```

As you can see, the variable `remainingMember` has three members that are the three members not explicitly called out before the rest. It means that the type of `remainingMember` is an object literal with a member `startTime`, `stopTime` and `time` of type Date, Date, and number.

Unleashing the Power of Type with Objects

Destructuring and rest also work with an array. You can specify a variable name that will be of the type of the array. The rest allows creating a new array with the remainder of the value with the type of the initial array. In the following code example, the `value1` contains the number 1 (not a string but as a number). The `value2` contains 2, and `value3To9` is an array with the values 3, 4, 5, 6, 7, 8, and 9:

```
const values = [1, 2, 3, 4, 5, 6, 7, 8, 9];
const [value1, value2, ...value3To9] = values;
```

It is also possible to skip position by using a comma without specifying a variable. In the following code example, there is a space between `value_1` and `value_2`, which means that the value at the second position, which is 2, is not in any individual variable (`value1` or `value2`), neither is in the variable `value4To9`:

```
const values = [1, 2, 3, 4, 5, 6, 7, 8, 9];
const [value1, value2, ...value3To9] = values;
const [value_1, , value_3, ...value4To9] = values;
```

Tuple

A **tuple** is an alternative to an object to hold multiple values within a single variable. Often used to move information around by function, it leverages an array to carry different types. The assignation with a tuple is done by setting the desired value in a specific index of an array, which the consumer must know to retrieve the pertinent information. In JavaScript, the usage of an array is sufficient. However, doing so in TypeScript leads to a weak type. The following code shows that TypeScript will infer the type to be an array of number or string, which can make sense but not when the code wants to be strongly typed. The reason is that an array can be a number or type at any position of the array, while in a tuple situation we want to have a specific type for each position in the array:

```
let tuple1 = ["First name", "Last Name", 1980]; // Infered as (string | number)[]
tuple1[2] = "Not a number";
let tuple2: [string, string, number] = ["First name", "Last Name", 1980];
// Tuple
tuple2[2] = "Not a number"; // Does not compile
```

To overcome the array inference, we need to specify the type for each position. However, even if a tuple is more specific than an array with multiple types because of the specification by the index of the type, this one still is not as safe as using an object:

```
let tuple3: [string, string, number]
tuple3 = ["Only One"]; // Does not compile
```

```
tuple3 = ["One", "Two", 3, "four"]; // Does not compile
tuple3[5] = "12"; // Compile
```

The previous code illustrates that during instantiation, there is a validation of type as well as a validation of size. It means that when assigning values, you must respect the type and the number of expected values. However, the last line of the code shows the nature of the array surface, and regardless of the fact that the tuple declaration specifies three positions, it is possible to add any type at any position after the ones defined. In the code example, the three first positions (index 0, 1, and 2) are strongly typed but position four and above can be anything. Nevertheless, changing a value, with the square brackets, will validate the type:

```
tuple3[5] = "12"; // Compile, do not mind the type
tuple3[1]= 2; // Does not compile, require to be a string
```

Tuple supports spread operator to deconstruct a function parameter into several variables. The following code example shows that a single tuple argument can be spread. The function `restFunction` is the equivalent of the `resultFunction`. The code example shows that it is possible to pass a tuple but not an array:

```
function restFunction(...args: [number, string, boolean]): void{
  const p1:number = args[0];
  const p2:string = args[1];
  const p3:boolean = args[2];
  // Code
}

function resultFunction(p1: number, p2: string, p3: boolean): void{
  // Code
}

let tuple4: [number, string, boolean] = [0, "one", false];
let array4: (number | string | boolean )[] = [0, "one", false];

restFunction(...tuple4);
restFunction(...array4); // Doesn't compile

restFunction(tuple4[0],tuple4[1],tuple4[2]);
restFunction(array4[0],array4[1],array4[2]); // Does not compile
```

Tuple supports optional. The syntax is similar to a function with optional parameters or a type with optional members. Positions without value are automatically set to `undefined`:

```
let tuple5: [number, string?, boolean?];
tuple5 = [1];
tuple5 = [1, "two"];
tuple5 = [1, "two", false];
```

The previous declaration is similar to the following, where optional position can be set to `undefined` as well:

```
let tuple5: [number, (string | undefined)?, (boolean | undefined)?]
```

Setting the tuple definition in a type can be advantageous when a tuple is reused in several places. The syntax is identical to when defining a type with the keyword type:

```
type MyTuple = [number, string];
let tuple6:MyTuple = [1, "Test"];
```

In conclusion, the tuple is a convenient way to pass information in a function and also to quickly return more than one value. However, a better alternative is to define a quick interface with the member desired. Not only does it not rely on position, but it can be reused in many situations easily by allowing extension and intersection. Furthermore, an object is easier to read because the assignation and the readability rely on a name instead of a number.

The differences between declare and let/const/var

It is possible to use `declare` instead of one of the three declarators `let`,`const`, and `var`. However, `declare` won't generate any JavaScript code during compilation and must be used in conjunction with `let`, `const` or `var`. The role of `declare` is to indicate to TypeScript's compiler that the variable exists but is defined somewhere else:

```
declare let myVariable: string;
```

The main role of `declare` is when signatures need to be defined. The use of `declare` in a definition file makes sense because it is only defining the type and not actually declaring the variable.

`declare` can be used to declare a module. Declaring a module is used to write a definition file outside the actual implementation of the code, which is written in JavaScript or TypeScript:

```
declare module "messageformat" {
}
```

Summary

In this chapter, we discussed many ways that generic information can be stored with the concept of many objects. We demystified the difference between the uppercase and lowercase object with an object literal and an instantiated object. We clarified two different structures to hold quick access data with index signature and map. The chapter continued with how to manipulate several types with a union and an intersection. Finally, we saw how to destruct, and how declare is different than the three previous declarations mentioned in `Chapter 2`, *Onboarding Types with Primitive*.

In the next chapter, we will see how to work with `object-oriented`. The next chapter covers how to use inheritance, encapsulation, and static function. The notions of interface and how to define a constructor signature in an interface will be explained. The next chapter dives into the powerful world of `object-oriented` in TypeScript.

4
Transforming Your Code into Object-Oriented

Object-oriented has its own set of jargon, and TypeScript relies on much of it. In this chapter, all the concepts of object-oriented that TypeScript supports are discussed with examples. We will see what a class is and how to instantiate a class into an object. We will also see how a constructor can be strongly typed with TypeScript, and how, with a shorthand syntax, we can assign a class's fields directly from the constructor. We will cover the principle of encapsulation with visibility, how to implement an interface, and how to bring abstraction to a class.

In this chapter, we will cover the following topics:

- What is a class and how do we define one?
- How type comes into play with a class's constructor
- What is encapsulation using `public`, `private`, and `protected`
- Reducing the definition of a field with a value set at construction time
- What is static?
- Use cases for a non-public constructor
- Using an object from a class versus an object literal
- How an interface can be useful in object-oriented
- Bringing abstraction with an abstract class
- How to have a property that is read-only
- Enforcing a specific constructor from an interface

What is a class and how do we define one?

At the core of object-oriented is the class. A class is a definition of what is available for an object once instantiated. A class holds variables and functions that were judged cohesive by the developer. A class can share information across all instances of the same class or have its own data, which is unique from the beginning of the life of the object until its death.

The creation of a class starts with the keyword `class` followed by the name of the class. It is similar to the creation of an interface:

```
export class MyClass {
}
```

A class can define variables and functions. Each of them is `public` by default, meaning that they are accessible from outside the class by the name of the instance:

```
export class Variables {
 public a: number = 1;
  private b: number = 2;
  protected c: number = 3;
  d: number = 4; // Also public
}
```

Once a class is defined, it can be instantiated. An instantiation means that a class becomes concrete and the life cycle for its content starts. To create an instance of a class, the `new` keyword must be used. After `new` comes the name of the class with parentheses:

```
const d = new Variables();
```

How type comes into play with a class's constructor

The instantiation of a class calls the constructor of the class. If this one is not defined, nothing is called. When no constructor is defined, the parentheses do not have any argument. The constructor's goal is to provide initialization of data to the class:

```
const d = new Variables();
```

In the case where the parameters are defined, the initialization must provide all the non-optional parameters. In the following code, the instantiation calls the constructor that has two parameters:

```
class MyClass {
    constructor(param1: number, param2: string) {
    }
}
const myClassInstance = new MyClass(1, "Must be present");
```

A constructor is similar to a function but cannot have an override. There is only a single constructor that can be defined. By default, it is public if no visibility is provided:

```
class MyClass {
   private m1: number;
   private m2: string;
   private m3: number;
   constructor(param1: number, param2: string) {
      this.m1 = param1;
      this.m2 = param2;
      this.m3 = 123;
   }
}
```

However, a constructor can be overloaded by many signatures. Similar to a function, the use of many definitions is possible with the use of a semicolon. In the following example, you can see that it is possible to instantiate the class with a single number or with a number and a string:

```
class ClassWithConstructorOverloaded {
  private p1: number;
  private p2: string;

  constructor(p1: number);
  constructor(p1: number, p2?: string) {
    this.p1 = p1;
    if (p2 === undefined) {
      p2 = "default";
    }
    this.p2 = p2;
  }
}
```

Transforming Your Code into Object-Oriented

If a class extends another class, it must call super with the parameter of the right type to the base class. The class that inherits the second class does not need to have the same number of constructor parameters, nor the same type. What is important is the call to super to respect the type of the extended class. In the following example, MyClass has a constructor that takes a number and a string. The class that extends MyClass, MyClass2, must call super with a number and a string. The example illustrates that the value can come from the constructor of the class or can be computed directly:

```
class MyClass2 extends MyClass {
    constructor(p1: number) {
       super(p1, "Here");
    }
}
```

What is encapsulation using public, private, and protected

The use of var, let, and const is not available at a class level. Class declares by using the public, private, and protected encapsulation visibility keywords. The scope is conscribed to the class with some minor difference between the three.

A class variable with the public keyword declaration allows the variable to be available inside and outside the class. The public modifier brings the instance of the class to allow it to read and write the value outside the class:

```
export class Variables {
    public a: number = 1;
}
const d = new Variables();
d.a = 100;
console.log(d.a);
```

On the other hand, the private declaration restrains the access to the class itself. This is true for reading and writing:

```
export class Variables {
    private b: number = 2;
}
const d = new Variables();
d.b = 100; // Not allowed, won't compile
console.log(d.b); // Not allowed, won't compile
```

Finally, a `protected` encapsulation is similar to `private` but it allows us to read and to write the value of the `protected` variable outside the class itself. However, the access is restricted to the class that declares the `protected` and the class that extends this one. A `protected` variable or function shares access down the hierarchy of classes. That means that all classes that inherit a class with `protected` members have access to the `protected` member:

```
class BaseClass {
  public a: number = 1;
  private b: number = 2;
  protected c: number = 3;
}

class ChildClass extends BaseClass {
  public d: number = 1;
  private e: number = 2;
  protected f: number = 3;
  public f1():void{
    super.a;
    super.c;
    this.a;
    this.c;
  }
}

const child = new ChildClass();
console.log(child.a);
console.log(child.d);
```

In the example, the child class has access to the base class members that are `public` and `protected`. Once the child class is instantiated, only `public` variables are available. Private members are only available in the class where they are defined. This is true for variables and functions.

Reducing the definition of a field with a value set at construction time

It can be cumbersome to always set values from the constructor to a field. A possibility is to assign the field directly from the constructor signature into the class:

```
class MyClass3{
  public constructor(private p1:number, public p2:string){}
}
```

```
const myClass3 = new MyClass3(1, "2");
console.log(myClass3.p2);
```

By setting the visibility of the encapsulation of each parameter of the constructor, a member is created with the same type. In the preceding example, two fields are created for the class with the name and the type of the parameter. The following code is exactly the same as the previous example, which is heavier in terms of definition and assignation:

```
class MyClass3Same {
  private p1: number;
  public p2: string;
  public constructor(p1: number, p2: string) {
    this.p1 = p1;
    this.p2 = p2;
  }
}

const myClass3Same = new MyClass3Same (1, "2");
console.log(myClass3.p2);
```

What is static?

A static member is a member that can be accessed without instantiating the class. Everything that is static is shared across all instances for the life of your system. Static variables and functions are associated with the class, not an instance of the class or a particular object. If you are coming from JavaScript, you can see static as being a member associated with the prototype chain instance of the instance.

Contrary to many other languages, TypeScript does not allow us to have a static class. It does not remove much, because if you need to have a static class, you just need to have the function directly inside the module instead of being in a class. If you want to have all your static classes inside a class and prevent the consumer of your library from instantiating the class, you can mark the class as abstract. An abstract class cannot be instantiated without being extended:

```
abstract class FakeStaticClass {
 public static m1: number;
 public static f1(): void { }
}

console.log(FakeStaticClass.m1);
FakeStaticClass.f1();

const instance1 = new FakeStaticClass(); // Doesn't compile
```

Static members can be from all encapsulation visibilities: `public`, `protected`, or `private`. However, only `public` visibility is accessible from outside the class. The `private` and `protected` are available within the class that defines the status members. A protected member can be accessed from a class that extends another class with static members:

```
class StaticClass {
  public static ps: number;
  private static privateStatic: number;
  protected static protecStatic: number;
}

StaticClass.ps = 1;
```

Only `public static` members are accessible from outside the class. The `private` and `protected` are accessible within the class. To use any static members, the name of the class must be specified before the use of the member. This rule is also needed when inside the class. The `this` pointer is only available within an instance, and since static is not part of any instance but part of `class`, it cannot be reached with the instance's `this` pointer:

```
class StaticClass {
  public static ps: number;
  private static privateStatic: number;
  protected static protecStatic: number;

  public nonStaticFunction():void{
    StaticClass.ps;
    StaticClass.privateStatic;
    StaticClass.protecStatic;
  }
}
```

Use cases for a non-public constructor

A `private` constructor revokes the possibility to instantiate the class from the outside. The following code does not compile because the constructor is `private`. The same would also be true if the constructor were `protected`:

```
class PrivateConstructor{
 private constructor(){
 }
}

const pc = new PrivateConstructor(); // Does not compile
```

In that case, the only way to instantiate the class is by using a `public static` function that creates the object of the type class and returns it. In the following code, the `private` constructor creates an instance; to access this instance, `GetInstance` is used, which is static and does not need to have an instance to be called:

```
class SingletonClass {
  private static instance: SingletonClass;
  private constructor() {
  SingletonClass.instance = new SingletonClass();
  }

  public static GetInstance(): SingletonClass {
    return SingletonClass.instance;
  }
}
const singletonClass = SingletonClass.GetInstance();
```

A known pattern is to have a `SingletonClass`. Only a single instance of the class exists and this control can be managed by having a single function that uses `new` once and then always returns the same instance. Another use case is to have a factory that creates all the instances.

Using an object from a class versus an object literal

An object literal is quick to build and does not need to have the data passed down a constructor or `public` members to fill an object. An object literal is an efficient way to move data around. You can read a JSON file, receive the data from an Ajax call or from many sources, and cast to the desired type:

```
ajax.then((response:any)=>{
    return response as DataTyped;
};
```

Chapter 4

However, if you have many functions or more complex logic that needs to be encapsulated, a class is more pragmatic. The reason is that using an object literal would require assigning the function on each instance manually. Also, a class can contain a `private` function that you may not want to expose, provide encapsulation with `private/protected` and interfaces. An object literal's fields are `public` and accessible. In the following example, we see data returned from an Ajax call. The expected type is `ObjectDefinition`, which has a function. The function doesn't come for free like with a class during the initialization. Hence, it must be attached to the object. In that case, we need to refer to a variable that has a function. This can be tedious with complex definitions:

```
interface ObjectDefinition {
  m1: string;
  funct1: () => void;
}

let ajax: any;
const funct1 = () => { };

ajax.then((response: any) => {
  const r = response as ObjectDefinition;
  r.funct1 = funct1;
  return r;
});
```

It is possible to reduce the burden of the previous example by having a `function` that builds each object literal by attaching the functions. In that case, the `function` returns the type of the object literal. This `function` acts as a constructor:

```
function createObj(m1: string): ObjectDefinitionClass {
  return {
    m1: m1,
    funct1: () => { }
  }
}

ajax.then((response: any) => {
  const r = response as Model;
  return createObj(r.m1);
});
```

Transforming Your Code into Object-Oriented

The same code with a class looks like the following code:

```
class ObjectDefinitionClass implements ObjectDefinition {
 public m1: string;
 public funct1(): void { }

 constructor(param1: string) {
   this.m1 = param1;
 }
}

ajax.then((response: any) => {
 const r = response as ObjectDefinition;
 return new ObjectDefinitionClass(r.m1);
});
```

In that particular case, what can be interesting is to divide the fields from the functions and pass all the fields by an interface in the constructor. Here is a third version using an interface for the variables and the functions:

```
interface Model {
 m1: string;
}

interface Funct {
 funct1: () => void;
}

class ObjectDefinitionClass2 implements Model, Funct {
 public m1: string;
 public funct1(): void { }
 constructor(param1: Model) {
   this.m1 = param1.m1;
 }
}

ajax.then((response: any) => {
 const r = response as Model;
 return new ObjectDefinitionClass2(r);
});
```

In terms of testability, a class has the advantage of allowing any of the members to be stubbed easily. Here is a simple example with the Jest library:

```
const forTesting = new ObjectDefinitionClass("1");
forTesting.funct1 = jest.fn();
```

How an interface can be useful in object-oriented

An interface serves many roles. We saw that you can define a contract for particular objects with an interface. However, interfaces can do much more.

An interface defines which members you want the consumer of your library to see and use. The `public`, `private`, and `protected` visibility keywords serve the same purpose. However, in some cases, you may need to have `public` members and still not allow everyone to use them. One reason can be that you want to have deep access to unit testing, hence having most of your members `public` allows you to black boxing functions testing. However, it might expose too much. Therefore, an interface can define every member that is accessible and be implemented by a class. Instead of passing the reference to the class directly, the interface is distributed externally while you can use the class internally:

```
class ClassA {
 public mainFunction(): void
{
   this.subFunction1();
   this.subFunction2();
 }

 private subFunction1(): void { }
 private subFunction2(): void { }
}
```

The class has two `private` functions that are executed by the main function, named `mainFunction`. However, the encapsulation does not allow us to unit test the `private` function without using some hack to access these functions. We want to avoid casting the main object to any to access the function because, if these functions change, the test might fail not because of wrong logic but because TypeScript was not able to refactor the function since the type was coerced to any. A better practice is to use an interface to keep the type present at all times:

```
interface IClassA {
 mainFunction(): void;
```

```
}

class ClassA2 implements IClassA {
 public mainFunction(): void {
    this.subFunction1();
    this.subFunction2();
 }

 public subFunction1(): void { }
 public subFunction2(): void { }
}
```

Everything is `public`, however, all the system is using `IClassA` instead of the class directly providing the encapsulation desired. The unit test can use the class and access the original `private` function.

A second case where the interface shines is that it allows us to have many concrete implementations of a specific type. You can define an interface that will be consumed by a function and has many implementations of this one. In the following example, we have a `consume` function that takes `IElement` as input. There are two concrete implementations of `IElement`, which gives the code the flexibility to have many element implementations. This help to reduce customized code in the consuming function by having a type that represents the minimum set of members needed to perform the task:

```
interface IElement {
 m1: string;
}

class E1 implements IElement { m1: string = "E1->m1"; a: number = 1; }
class E2 implements IElement { m1: string = "E2->m1"; b: boolean = true; }

class ClassB {
 public consume(element: IElement): void { }
}
```

Bringing abstraction with an abstract class

Abstraction is an object-oriented concept that allows us to have a base class that delegates the implementation of a function to the class that extends the `abstract` class.

The following example creates the main class by instantiating the custom logic class. It invokes the main function, which will execute the abstract function. To the MainClass class, the abstract function is a black box. It only knows its name, parameter types, and returns types. The example executes the commented block code A-C-B in that particular order:

```
abstract class MainClass {
  public mainCoreLogic(): void {
    // Code here [A]
    this.delegatedLogic();
    // Code here [B]
  }

  public abstract delegatedLogic(): void;

}


class CustomLogic extends MainClass {

  public delegatedLogic(): void {
    // Do some custom logic here [C]
  }

}

const c: MainClass = new CustomLogic();
c.mainCoreLogic();
```

The abstract is powerful when you pass a computed value to the abstract class and that this one also returns a result of a custom computation. Here is a second version that shows how two different implementations can occur while the main class remains unchanged. The main class is now named Calculus and has a public function that takes two numbers and returns a Boolean. It does some operations on the parameters and calls the delegated logic. The treatment of the value is unknown to the main class. The significant part of the operation is the result that is then used. On the side of the class that consumes the abstract class by extending the class. It has to provide all abstract functions or fields. Every abstract member becomes a public field at the extended level. In the example, the logic multiplies the two values that return the specified type:

```
abstract class Calculus {
  public isAboveZero(a: number, b: number): boolean {
    const positiveA = Math.abs(a);
    const positiveB = Math.abs(b);
    const result = this.delegatedLogic(positiveA, positiveB);
    return result > 0;
```

Transforming Your Code into Object-Oriented

```
  }

  public abstract delegatedLogic(a: number, b: number): number;
}

class AddLogic extends Calculus {
  public delegatedLogic(a: number, b: number): number {
    return a * b;
  }
}

const multi: Calculus = new AddLogic();
multi.isAboveZero(1, 2);
```

The code could have been written in a non-object-oriented way by providing by parameter the logic to execute. Here is the same version of the code without an `abstract`:

```
class CalculusWithoutAbstract {
  public constructor(private delegatedLogic: (a: number, b: number) => number) {
  }

  public isAboveZero(a: number, b: number): boolean {
    const positiveA = Math.abs(a);
    const positiveB = Math.abs(b);
    const result = this.delegatedLogic(positiveA, positiveB);
    return result > 0;
  }
}

const multi2: CalculusWithoutAbstract = new CalculusWithoutAbstract((a, b) => a * b);
multi2.isAboveZero(1, 2);
```

The version without an `abstract` takes in the constructor of the class the function to be called instead of the abstract function. The substitution between the two is a matter of preference. The main difference between the two is that using abstract force the `abstract` implementation to be public when the delegate function can remain `private`. However, the way to work around the visibility issue is to initialize with the base class instead of the child class:

```
const multi: Calculus = new AddLogic(); // Expose only the main function
const multi: AddLogic = new AddLogic(); // Expose the delegate function
```

How to have a property that is read-only

Read-only fields can be initialized once and don't need to be changed during the lifetime of the instance. The `readonly` keyword can be used in an interface to specify that once the field is set, the value doesn't change:

```
interface I1 {
  readonly id: string;
  name: string;
}

let i1: I1 = {
  id: "1",
  name: "test"
}

i1.id = "123"; // Does not compile
```

It can be at the class level where the value can be only set directly at the declaration or in the constructor. When a value is initialized next to the field's declaration, this one can still be redefined by the constructor. The following example shows this edge case. However, it is possible to only set it at declaration or just at the `constructor` level, which is often the case:

```
class C1 {
  public readonly id: string = "C1";

  constructor() {
    this.id = "Still can change";
  }

  public f1(): void {
    this.id = 1; // Doesn't compile
  }
}
```

Read-only with `static` can be useful to have constant for a particular class. The use of `const` is not allowed at a class level. If you want to centralize a value in the context of a particular class, the use of `public`, `static`, and `readonly` is an acceptable pattern:

```
class C2 {
  public static readonly MY_CONST: string = "TEST";
  public codeHere(): void {
    C2.MY_CONST;
  }
}
```

Enforcing a specific constructor from an interface

This is tricky because you cannot enforce by an interface the shape of a constructor. However, you can use an interface to ensure a class passed by the parameter has a specific constructor. The process requires two interfaces. One is the return type of the construction, and one is the interface used in the parameter:

```
interface ConstructorReturnType {
  member1: number;
  funct(): void;
}
interface EntityConstructor {
  new(value: number): ConstructorReturnType;
}
```

The first interface in this example has two members: one field and one function. The definition of the interface doesn't matter, it can be anything you want to get an instance of the function. The second interface has a constructor function, known as *newable*. It uses the `new` keyword with the input parameters and what it needs to create. The type should be the first interface created:

```
function entityFactory(ctor: EntityConstructor, value: number): ConstructorReturnType {
    return new ctor(value);
}
```

The next step is to create a function that takes the `newable` function and sets it as a parameter type. Optionally, you can have more parameters. In the example, a value for the constructor is passed. The return type of the function must be the type that the `newable` function returns. In this function, you can call `new` followed by the parameter of the interface that has the definition of the `newable` function. The code instantiates an instance of the class passed by the parameter. Only classes that respect the type contract of the `newable` function are accepted:

```
class Implementation1 implements ConstructorReturnType {

  public member1: number;

  constructor(value: number) {
    this.member1 = value;
  }

  public funct(): void {
```

```
    }

  }
  let impl1 = entityFactory(Implementation1, 1);
```

In the preceding code, the `Implementation1` class implements the returned implementation, hence will be a candidate for this function. It also has the constructor that takes a single-number parameter that will be invoked by the function.

On the other hand, the following code does not compile because the class does not inherit the returned type defined by the `newable` function:

```
  class Implementation2 {
     constructor(value: number) { }
  }

  let impl2 = entityFactory(Implementation2, 1);
```

An example that might not look valid but that compiles is the following code. It extends the returned class but does not respect the `newable` function argument that requires it to have a value. It is valid because the definition is only about the returned object and not the constructor. The constructor is called with a parameter, but the class doesn't have to handle it. In the following code, printing the `arguments` variable shows that it has the `1` value passed as the first parameter even if not explicitly required by the class:

```
  class Implementation3 implements ConstructorReturnType {
    public member1: number = 1;
    constructor() {
      console.log(arguments);
    }

    public funct(): void {
    }
  }

  let impl3 = entityFactory(Implementation3, 1);
```

Summary

In this chapter, we visited many object-oriented features. TypeScript is closing the gap with well-known programming languages that are object-oriented such as C# or Java. TypeScript, being a superset of JavaScript, must palliate some weakness of JavaScript in this regard but finish with its head-up with many features that are acceptable to write a professional application in an object-oriented fashion.

We saw how to work with encapsulation, which allows us to control the visibility of fields and functions. We discussed ways to strongly type a constructor, as well as how to use an interface to be implemented by a class. Within a class, we saw how to have static functions and abstraction functions. The next chapter will cover how we can identify precisely which type, object, or variable we are manipulating, allowing us to leverage specific members that are unique to each of them. We will see how to use JavaScript typecheckers, such as `typeof` and `instanceof`, and how to pattern with discriminator and defined guard for a structured type.

5
Scoping Variables with Different Patterns

In this chapter, we see the most basic concept that is a variable. Knowing what is the exact type, from a primitive to an object, is essential for accessing specific members. Scoping down the exact type at runtime and design time is crucial, to have consistency between the two environments and to have feedback about what is possible and what is not. The variety of configurations among the different types of variable requires many different patterns that are covered in this chapter.

This chapter will cover the following:

- How to compare at runtime and design time with `typeof`
- How to check with a guarantee for `undefined` and `null`
- Do I need to check every possibility of a union to have the right type?
- What is the limitation of `instanceof`?
- Why a discriminator is essential for type identification
- Why using `user` defined `guard`
- How and why to cast
- What is a type assertion?
- How to compare classes
- How to narrow type for function with a union in signatures

Comparing at runtime and design time with typeof

TypeScript brings type in JavaScript, but this is mostly true at design type. TypeScript during compilation removes all the type. This is the reason that the code produced is purely JavaScript and does not contain any trace of interfaces or types. The purity of respect for JavaScript makes type comparison harder because it cannot rely on the name of the type to perform a type check. However, we can use all JavaScript's tricks to know whether a value is from a different type. The first feature answers the main question of this section about how to compare runtime and design type. The use of the JavaScript `typeof` operator that is present in JavaScript is also working the same way in TypeScript. The `typeof` operator returns the type of a primitive, or it returns `object`.

The usage is simple: call `typeof` followed by the variable that you want to compare it with. Most of the time, you will compare it to the name of the type that requires being written in a string:

```
const a = "test";
let b: number = 2;
const c: boolean = true;
let d: number | string = "test";
console.log(typeof a); // string
console.log(typeof b); // number
console.log(typeof c); // boolean
console.log(typeof d); // string
```

The `typeof` operator is especially used when having a union type where an object can be from many primitives. In fact, it can be used even with a union that has a complex object (interface or type) because `typeof` returns `object`:

```
const e: number | string | { complex: string, obj: number } = { complex: "c", obj: 1 };
console.log(typeof e); // object
```

To know which type of object the object is will require the use of other mechanisms that we will cover in this chapter. Before moving on, even if `typeOf` is comparable to a string, the result of the operation can be set a type:

```
let f: number = 2;
if (typeof f === "number") {
    console.log("This is for sure a number");
}
type MyNewType = typeof f;
```

Note that `typeOf` works on primitive types but behaves strangely with `undefined` or `null`. However, `undefined` will return `undefined` and `null` will return `object`. The best approach to check for `undefined` or `null` is to not use `typeof`:

```
let g: number | undefined = undefined;
let h: number | undefined | null = null;
console.log(typeof g);
console.log(typeof h);
```

Differentiating undefined from null

While `typeof` returns the `undefined` string when performing against an undefined type, it returns `object` against `null`. This inconsistency becomes an issue when you forget which case can use `typeof` by performing the wrong operation for the wrong no type type. However, `undefined` and `null` do not require the use of `typeof` to do a type check. It is possible to compare directly the variable against `undefined` or `null`:

```
let g: number | undefined = undefined;
let h: number | undefined | null = null;
console.log(typeof g); // undefined
console.log(typeof h); // object
console.log(g === undefined); // true
console.log(g === null); // false
console.log(h === undefined); // false
console.log(h === null); // true
```

In a situation where a variable can be undefined or null or any other primitive, the best way is to check for the nullability of the type and carry on with further type comparisons.

Getting the type of element in a union

The TypeScript inference system gets better with every version. In the most recent version, TypeScript uses a control flow to find out in a smart way the type depending on how the code is written. If a check is performed in one code path, TypeScript knows that for the closure of the type validation that the type is as checked. If an *else* code path exists to a type check, it knows that it is the reverse of the type comparison.

The following code example shows that depending on the position of the execution the type changes. It starts as a number or undefined. The value check against `undefined` makes the value narrow down to an undefined value for the scope of the `if`. The `else` can only be everything else than undefined in the union. In that particular case, it can only be a number. After `if` and `else`, TypeScript cannot know what the type is; thus, the value is back to both potential types:

```
function myFunction(value: number | undefined): void {
 console.log("Value is number or undefined");
 if (value === undefined) {
 console.log("Value is undefined");
 } else {
 console.log("Value is NOT undefined, hence a number");
 }
 console.log("Value is number or undefined");
}
```

TypeScript understands the code flow. It is smart to freeze the type from a particular type check. In the following code example, a value equals to undefined force the function to return. It means that passing that point, there is no way to have an undefined value. The subtraction of `undefined` in the set of potential values diminishes the possibility to only a number:

```
function myFunction2(value: number | undefined): void {
 console.log("Value is number or undefined");
 if (value === undefined) {
 return;
 }
 console.log("Value is NOT undefined, hence a number");
}
```

TypeScript narrows down the union from your conditional check for more than a primitive. You can also use this behavior with a discriminator and a user-defined type guard, which are two patterns that we will see in this chapter.

The limitations of instanceof

Similar to `typeof`, there is in JavaScript the `instanceof` operator. The limitation of `instanceof` is that it can be only used on a type with a prototype chain: a class. Like `typeof`, `instanceof` works at design and runtime and is native to JavaScript:

```
class MyClass1 {
 member1: string = "default";
 member2: number = 123;
```

```
}
class MyClass2 {
  member1: string = "default";
  member2: number = 123;
}
const a = new MyClass1();
const b = new MyClass2();
if (a instanceof MyClass1) {
  console.log("a === MyClass1");
}
if (b instanceof MyClass2) {
  console.log("b === MyClass2");
}
```

Contrary to typeof, the result of instanceof is not a string and cannot be used in the console.log function; it is possible to set the value in a type or in a variable. It can only be used for comparison purposes. The next example does not compile:

```
type MyType = instanceOf MyClass1;
```

The instanceOf limitations are beyond just being focused on class. The instanceOf operator also does not distinguish which class is exactly used in the situation of inheritance. In the next code example, the variable c is of type MyClass3, which inherits MyClass2. InstanceOf identifies the variable to be of both types. In the following code, both if are entered:

```
class MyClass3 extends MyClass2 {
  member3: boolean = true;
}
const c = new MyClass3();
if (c instanceof MyClass2) {
  console.log("c === MyClass2");
}
if (c instanceof MyClass3) {
  console.log("c === MyClass3");
}
```

Using of a discriminator for type identification

TypeScript is a structural language, which means that it does not rely on the name of the type like a nominal language. JavaScript doesn't have a type; hence, it is a structural language. C# or Java are both nominal languages. The difference is important because it means that TypeScript doesn't check for the name of the interface or type to take any decision. This makes sense when we think about how TypeScript compiles the code. During compilation, all types are stripped out of the code to produce a clean JavaScript. This symbiosis is in respect to JavaScript; thus, giving TypeScript the honor of being a superset of JavaScript. However, at runtime for TypeScript and design time for JavaScript, we need to know which type we are manipulating. In structural code, the approach is to analyze, compare, and infer type by looking at the structure. If specific members exist, it gives a hint of what we are working on. The following code example shows two identical interfaces with the same body, a type with the same structure as well, and the first variable with an anonymous type. The object can be of each type because it respects the contract of each one:

```
interface Type1 {
  m1: string;
}
interface Type2 {
  m1: string;
}
type Type3 = { m1: string };
const v0 = { m1: "AllTheSame" };
const v1: Type1 = v0;
const v2: Type2 = v0;
const v3: Type3 = v0;
```

In the previous example, the way to make every type different is with the concept of a discriminator. A **discriminator** is a member with a shared name between a group of a common type that needs to be distinguished. This group is often a union. The idea is to have a unique `string literal` per type with the same name. Having `string literal` as a type member requires the implementation to implement the same `string`. It means that each instance of a specific type will have the same `string`. TypeScript can then infer the type by looking at `string literal`. The following code example applies this principle. The common member is named `kind`, and each interface and type has a unique one. The anonymous type tries to impersonate `Type1` but fails because the type inferred is a `string` and not a `string literal`:

```
interface Type1 {
```

```
  kind: "Type1";
  m1: string;
}

interface Type2 {
  kind: "Type2";
  m1: string;
}

type Type3 = { kind: "Type3"; m1: string };
const v0 = { kind: "Type1", m1: "AllTheSame" };
const v1: Type1 = v0; // Does not compile
const v2: Type2 = v0; // Does not compile
const v3: Type3 = v0; // Does not compile
```

The discriminator proves to be useful not only for avoid cross type but also for narrowing down a type. In a union of many types, when comparing against the discriminator, TypeScript will know exactly the type and hence the scope of the comparison. The following code allows reducing to the exact type. In that particular case, the m1 member is a member that is in all three types and thus does not require to be narrowed down to a single type to be used:

```
function threeLogic(param: Type1 | Type2 | Type3): void {
  switch (param.kind) {
    case "Type1":
      console.log(param.m1); // param is type Type1
    break;
    case "Type2":
      console.log(param.m1); // param is type Type2
    break;
    case "Type3":
      console.log(param.m1); // param is type Type3
    break;
  }
}
```

If we have an interface with completely different members, the distinction is primordial to have access to a member that is unique to one interface or another. The following code narrows down the interface, allowing it to use a member from the proper type, depending on the comparison:

```
interface Alpha { kind: "Alpha", alpha: string }
interface Beta { kind: "Beta", beta: string }

function AlphaBeta(param: Alpha | Beta): void {
  switch (param.kind) {
    case "Alpha":
```

Scoping Variables with Different Patterns

```
    console.log(param.alpha);
  break;
  case "Beta":
    console.log(param.beta);
  break;
  }
}
```

The usage of a string literal as a discriminator is often named the **literal type guard** or the **tagged union**. It is powerful for functional programming and provides a quick way to identify a type without having to develop specific conditions as needed in other techniques such as a user-defined guard.

The user-defined guard pattern

Knowing the type of an interface or type can be challenging. We saw in this chapter the use of a discriminator. However, there is a drawback with the commonly named `string literal` approach, which is with inheritance and intersection. The following code does not compile:

```
interface Type1 extends Type2 {
  kind: "Type1"; // Does not compile, expect "Type2"
  m1: number;
}

interface Type2 {
  kind: "Type2";
  m2: string;
}
```

The same is true with an intersection:

```
interface Type2 {
 kind: "Type2";
 m2: string;
}

interface Type3 {
 kind: "Type3";
 m3: string;
}

type Type4 = Type2 & Type3;
const type4: Type4 = { kind: ???, m2: "1", m3: "2" }; // Does not compile
```

The last code example creates for the member kind a type that requires to be both `strings literal` at the same time make it impossible to fulfill and not practical. With that information to hand, we can see that the discriminator pattern works well when inheritance is avoided as well as intersecting. The idea is to use a custom user-defined guard per type. This can be cumbersome to create but will ensure you the type at design and runtime. The idea is to check for fields and see whether they are defined. This technique works well for a type with no optional field, since you need to check whether fields exist. As the author of the function and the type, you do not need to check every field. You should know which field is enough to identify the type. In the following code, both types exist, and one type extends the other. Two type user-defined guards are created—one for each interface:

```
interface Type1 extends Type2 {
  m1: number;
}

interface Type2 {
  m2: string;
  m3: number;
}

function checkInterfaceICheck1(obj: any): obj is Type1 {
  const type1WithMaybeManyUndefinedMembers = (obj as Type1);
  return type1WithMaybeManyUndefinedMembers.m1 !== undefined
  && type1WithMaybeManyUndefinedMembers.m2 !== undefined
  && type1WithMaybeManyUndefinedMembers.m3 !== undefined
}

function checkInterfaceICheck2(obj: any): obj is Type2 {
  const type1WithMaybeManyUndefinedMembers = (obj as Type2);
  return type1WithMaybeManyUndefinedMembers.m2 !== undefined
  && type1WithMaybeManyUndefinedMembers.m3 !== undefined;
}

function codeWithUnionParameter(obj: Type1 | Type2): void {
  if (checkInterfaceICheck1(obj)) {
  console.log("Type1", obj.m1);
  }

  if (checkInterfaceICheck2(obj)) {
  console.log("Type2", obj.m2);
  }
}
```

Scoping Variables with Different Patterns

The function must know which of the two types are passed, and it checks by using the user-defined guard. The return type of the defined guard is unique. It uses the name of the parameter followed by *is* and the type we are expecting if the value is `true`. It allows to automatically narrow down to the expected type by comparing the structure. If everything is present and defined, it returns `true`, but the function will not return an actual `boolean` value. It returns the object cast to the type.

The reason to cast a type

Casting is the act of taking one type and transposing it onto something else. It is dangerous and should be used seldomly. The reason casting can have side effects is that you are taking manual control of coercing a variable into another type. The type may be creating an incompatible and unexpected result. A cast is possible for any kind of variable, from a primitive to a more-complex object.

The most basic cast scenario is getting a value that is from `any` and to type it. The following code shows a number that is set in `any` and then cast to a variable of type number. You can notice two different ways to cast. One with the smaller and bigger symbol `<>` and one with `as`. The latter is the recommended way because it does not confuse code using TSX syntax, which uses the symbols for a component:

```
let something: any = 1;
let variable1: number;
variable1 = <number>something;
variable1 = something as number;
```

The previous code works because the cast went from `any` to `number`. Casting a number to a string does not work. The reason is that cast only works if you are working with a subtype. Furthermore, `any` is a subtype of everything, which allows casting to every type. However, the following code does not compile because `variable1` is a number that is cast to a string:

```
let variable1: number = 1;
let variable2: string = variable1 as string;
```

TypeScript is also present to avoid casting between objects that miss fields. In the following code, both types cannot be cast to each other. TypeScript cannot find `m2` in `Type1`, and the second cast cannot find `m1` in the following code:

```
interface Type1 {
  m1: number;
}

interface Type2 {
```

```
  m2: string;
  m3: number;
}

let t1: Type1 = { m1: 123 };
let t2: Type2 = t1 as Type2; // Property 'm2' is missing in type 'Type1'
let t3: Type2 = { m2: "2", m3: 3 };
let t4: Type1 = t2 as Type1;// Property 'm1' is missing in type 'Type2'
```

However, adding m1 to Type2 changes the whole situation and allows casting in both sides without any compilation errors. The reason is that Type1 is a subtype of Type2 by its structure, which is what matters in TypeScript:

```
interface Type1 {
  m1: number;
}

interface Type2 {
  m1: number;
  m2: string;
  m3: number;
}

let t1: Type1 = { m1: 123 };
let t2: Type2 = t1 as Type2;
let t3: Type2 = { m1: 1, m2: "2", m3: 3 };
let t4: Type1 = t2 as Type1;
```

What is interesting about the last code is that the last cast is useless. The reason is that Type2 has all the structure of Type1, and Type1 is a subtype of Type2. It means that they are structurally equivalent at a minimum point in their structure:

```
let t3: Type2 = { m1: 1, m2: "2", m3: 3 };
let t4: Type1 = t2;
```

The casting is required for t1 to Type2 because t1 doesn't fulfil the contract (it misses m2 and m3). The cast produces a false Type2 because m2 and m3 are not there, which means they are undefined. Type2 does not have any undefined type for these members, which makes it problematic for future usage, since TypeScript will allow m2 to use any string's function while this one is undefined. The casting comes with great responsibilities, and the tampering type will make TypeScript unable to perform safe validation.

The slippery slope is steeper when a cast is affecting an object that is any. It's hard to avoid all any. For example, when data is crossing between systems. An Ajax request returns a JSON object, which is an inevitability, as any. The response is not typed, and to introduce the value into TypeScript, a crucial cast is performed.

Scoping Variables with Different Patterns

A bad pattern is to cast to `any` and then to the desired type. This is a way to short-circuit TypeScript, finding that the cast is not a valid one. Everything can be cast to `any` and from any cast to everything else:

```
let a: number = 1;
let b: string = "2";
a = b as number; // Doesn't compile
a = b as any as number; //Shortcircuit with any
```

What is a type assertion?

There are scenarios where you know that a type is not undefined or null but that TypeScript will hint that it might be. When this happens, you can perform a check against `undefined` or `null` and within the closure of the condition will be a guarantee that the type is not nullable. However, three scenarios can benefit from having a shorter syntax.

The first scenario is with a deep-nesting object. In that case, you may have several levels of nullable fields and if you are sure that they are not undefined or null, this will be great to avoid having a nested `if` structure:

```
interface T1 {
 myNumber: number | undefined;
}

interface T2 {
 t1: T1 | undefined;
}

interface T3 {
 t2: T2 | undefined;
}

const myObject: T3 | undefined = {
 t2: {
 t1: {
  myNumber: 1
 }
 }
}

if (myObject !== undefined) {
 if (myObject.t2 !== undefined) {
  if (myObject.t2.t1 !== undefined) {
   if (myObject.t2.t1.myNumber !== undefined) {
    console.log("My number is :", myObject.t2.t1.myNumber);
```

```
        }
      }
    }
}
```

The conditional check is the safest way to ensure that nothing is undefined. However, in some cases, the check may have been made prior to accessing the data, but an access to the value is needed outside the scope of the check, which makes TypeScript nervous about `if` meanwhile, the state has changed. That would be the case if we tried to access `myNumber` right after the previous code. This is where `assertion` type comes into play. A `assertion` type is the bang operator, or exclamation point, after a member that specifies that the member is not null or undefined. You are asserting that this is the case and take the responsibility to *un-undefined* or to *un-nullable* to field.

It means that you can access the member by using a single line:

```
console.log("My number is :", myObject!.t2!.t1!.myNumber);
```

It is crucial to understand that this can lead to a potential runtime error if used at the wrong time. For some reason, any nullable field can become nullable if applied at the wrong time or place. There is no guarantee that the execution will succeed but will soothe TypeScript error saying that you are accessing a nullable field without narrowing it down to the type.

The second case of using type `assertion` is when you are defining a field in a class. If TypeScript is set to have the compilation strictness to avoid an uninitialized field, then you will have an error when defining a field and not specifying a value at the declaration or in the constructor. This is a great validation, but, in some rare cases, the value may come later in an `initialize` function. In that case, you can assert the class's field to say that you are taking care of the value:

```
class LateInitialization {
  m1!: number; // Not initialized (use type assertion)
  constructor() {
    // No initializing here
  }
  public init(): void {
    this.m1 = 1;
  }
}
```

Scoping Variables with Different Patterns

Once again, this should be used with parsimony, because it can bring some issues. For example, you can now access the member and use it without TypeScript validating that the value was assigned before accessing the value:

```
constructor() {
   this.m1 + 1; // This will fail
}
```

This might seem like a trifle, since you know that you will not do such a thing. But it can be less obvious. A case of error is that you are accessing the member from another public function that might be called before the `init` function causing any usage of the variable to be undefined. Type asserting forces TypeScript to close its eyes about uninitialized value.

The last scenario is also dangerous to use and should be coded only with a lot of care. You can at any time use the exclamation point to erase the nullability. It means that it works with a simple variable as well. The following code declares a variable of type string or undefined. It sets its value using a function that is immediately invoked. The function has a return type of also `string | undefined`. TypeScript concludes that this function may return one or both types, and hence could legally return something undefined. However, we know that it is not the case, and hence can use the exclamation point to remove the undefined possibility and use the string's functions:

```
let var1: string | undefined;
var1 = ((): string | undefined => "Not undefined but type is still both")();
console.log(var1!.substr(0, 5));
```

Again, this is dangerous and a better way around it could be employed. The first thing is to avoid having a union with `undefined` or `null`. If this is out of your control, avoiding functions such as one of the last code examples that aslo return undefined. The same code with the return type of string would have solved the problem gracefully.

Comparing classes

Classes are different than interfaces, types, or primitives. They have a prototype chain and obey different rules. For example, two different classes can be interchangeable if they have the same structure. The following classes, `C1` and `C2`, are identical in terms of structure and can be swapped in the function that requires `C1`. You can even instantiate `C2` in a `C1` variable:

```
class C1 {
  public a: number = 1;
  public funct(): void { }
```

```
}

class C2 {
  public a: number = 1;
  public funct(): void { }
}

const c1: C1 = new C1();
const c2: C2 = new C2();
const c12: C1 = new C2();

function executeClass1(c1: C1): void {
  c1.funct();
}

executeClass1(c1);
executeClass1(c2);
executeClass1(c12);
```

If we add in the `private` field in `C1` or `C2`, then it won't be the same:

```
class C1 {
  public a: number = 1;
  public funct(): void { }
  private p: string = "p";
}

class C2 {
  public a: number = 1;
  public funct(): void { }
  private p: string = "p";
}

const c1: C1 = new C1();
const c2: C2 = new C2();
const c12: C1 = new C2(); // Does not compile

function executeClass1(c1: C1): void {
  c1.funct();
}

executeClass1(c1);
executeClass1(c2); // Does not compile
executeClass1(c12);
```

The `private` and `protected` fields make each class unique. TypeScript continues to compare the structure but does make an exception with regard to these two visibility modifiers.

Scoping Variables with Different Patterns

The reason is when using inheritance and assigning a child class to a base type it must be from the same hierarchy and not something with a similar shape that is not from the same hierarchy. The following code shows how without a `private` or a `protected` field the base class can be substituted by a single class that has the structure of the child and the base:

```
class B1 {
   public baseFunct(): void { }
}

class C1 extends B1 {
   public a: number = 1;
   public funct(): void { }
}

class C2 {
   public a: number = 1;
   public funct(): void { }
   public baseFunct(): void { }
}

const c1: B1 = new C1();
const c2: B1 = new C2();
```

However, adding a `private` field at the base class `B1` and the same in `C2` makes them different, which stops `C2` being addressable to the variable `C2` of type `B1`:

```
class B1 {
 private name: string = "b1";
 public baseFunct(): void { }
}

class C1 extends B1 {
 public a: number = 1;
 public funct(): void { }
}

class C2 {
 private name: string = "c2";
 public a: number = 1;
 public funct(): void { }
 public baseFunct(): void { }
}

const c1: B1 = new C1();
const c2: B1 = new C2(); // Does not compile
```

Narrowing type for function with a union in signatures

Complex functions can be hard to work with. This is often the case with a function with one or many parameters of different types, which can also return one or several types. TypeScript allows stitching any type together:

```
function f(p: number | string): boolean | Date {
  if (typeof p === "number") {
    return true;
  }
  return new Date();
}

const r1: boolean = f(1); // Does not compile
const r2: Date = f("string"); // Does not compile
```

In the previous code, the code is not compiling. The reason is because the function returns a union that must narrow down. However, if we add the overloads above the function, we can match the union to one particular set of parameters to a single return type. The previous code was not compiling because it was returning a union into a single type variable. With a change specifying that when a parameter is a number, then the function returns boolean, and when it is a string it returns a date, no casting or anything is required:

```
function f(p: number): boolean;
function f(p: string): Date;
function f(p: number | string): boolean | Date {
  if (typeof p === "number") {
    return true;
  }
  return new Date();
}

const r1: boolean = f(1);
const r2: Date = f("string");
```

This is beyond just associating a single parameter to a return type. For example, in the following code, we make sure we can only send all number parameters together or all strings together:

```
function g(p: number, q: number): boolean;
function g(p: string, q: string): Date;
function g(p: number | string, q: number | string): void {
}
```

```
g(1, "123"); // Doesn't compile
g(1, 2);
g("1", "2");
```

Summary

In this chapter, we covered how to have a better sense of the type of a variable. Not only does it help to take decisions, but it narrows down to a single type, giving the possibility to access specific members that are specific to a particular type.

In the next chapter, we will see how to generalize a type by using a generic variable. Generic variables increase the reusability of objects and variables in your code, which reduces the necessity of creating trivial types.

6
Reusing Code Through Generic

This chapter is built from notions introduced by the previous chapters. The chapter built on top of notions by enhancing type by making them generic. Basic topics such as defining a generic class and interface are covered. Through the chapter, we move into more advanced topics such as generic constraints are part of the content. The goal of this chapter is to make your code more generic to increase the reusability of your classes, functions, and structures, to reduce the burden of duplicating code.

The content in this chapter covers the following:

- How generic can make your code reusable
- Accepted kinds of data structure for generic type
- How to constrain the generic type
- Generic and intersection
- Default generic
- Generic optional type
- Generic constraints with a union type
- Restricting string choices with `keyof`
- Limiting the access to members of a generic type
- Reducing your type creation with a mapped type
- Generic type in TSX file

Generic code to increase reusability

Generic is available in almost all typed language. It allows transforming your code in a reusable fashion without having to rely on unsafe casting to retrieve the value stored in an object. Without generic, there are different ways to achieve reusability. For example, you can have an interface with an `any` type.

Reusing Code Through Generic

That would make the field open to receive any kind of object, hence being reusable for many scenarios:

```
interface ReusableInterface1 {
    entity: any;
}
```

A slightly better way would be to specify whether we want to accept primitives or only objects:

```
interface ReusableInterface2 {
    entity: object;
}

const ri2a: ReusableInterface2 = { entity: 1 }; // Does not compile
const ri2b: ReusableInterface2 = { entity: { test: "" } };
```

In both cases, the problem comes when we want to use the reusable field. The same result occurs with `any` or `object`, which is that we do not have access to the original variable's member because we do not have a way to know what was the original type:

```
const value = ri2b.entity; // value -> "object"
```

In this code, it is impossible to use `.test` of the entity without casting back to the entity. In that particular type, it is an anonymous type but still possible:

```
const valueCasted = value as { test: string };
console.log(valueCasted.test);
```

However, generic can remove this hinder to access the original type by bringing the type of the object into the definition of the type without tampering the type to be isolated with a single type. To create a generic function, interface, or class, you need to use the smaller or bigger sign, < >:

```
interface MyCustomTypeA {
    test: string;
}

interface MyCustomTypeB {
    anything: boolean;
}

interface ReusableInterface3<T> {
    entity: T;
}
```

The name between the brackets does not matter. In the following code, we are using the entity with two custom interfaces and use them as type T. We are also using a number directly. We can use all the possible types because we do not have a generic constraint, yet, in place:

```
const ri3a: ReusableInterface3<MyCustomTypeA> = { entity: { test: "yes" } };
const ri3b: ReusableInterface3<MyCustomTypeB> = { entity: { anything: true } };
const ri3c: ReusableInterface3<number> = { entity: 1 };
```

The biggest advantage is that if we access the object, the field entity is of a T type, which changes depending on how the object was created:

```
console.log(ri3a.entity.test); // "yes" -> string
console.log(ri3b.entity.anything); // true -> boolean
console.log(ri3c.entity); // 1 -> number
```

Accepted kinds of data structure for generic type

The concept of generic spreads beyond just interfaces. Generic is available for types but also with classes, and it can transform a function as well. The disposition of the brackets that define the generic type goes right after the interface name, type, or the class name. We will see later that it must also go after the name of a function. Generic can be used to have a generic field, generic parameter, generic return type, and generic variable:

```
type MyTypeA<T> = T | string; // Type

interface MyInterface<TField, YField> { // Interface wiht two types
  entity1: TField;
  myFunction(): YField;
}

class MyClass<T>{ // Class
 list: T[] = [];
 public displayFirst(): void {
   const first: T = this.list[0]; // Variable
   console.log(first);
 }
}
```

A generic type can have many generics at the same time, allowing multiple fields or function parameters to have a different kind of type:

```
function extractFirstElement<T, R>(list: T[], param2: R): T {
  console.log(param2);
  return list[0];
}
```

Constaining a generic type

In a previous code example in this chapter, we used the type object to make sure no primitives were passed in an interface. The problem with the use of an object is that you do not get back the initial type when you get back the entity. The following code illustrates the problem:

```
interface ReusableInterface2 {
  entity: object;
}

const a = {
  what: "ever"
};

const c: ReusableInterface2 = { entity: a };
console.log(c.entity.what); // Does not compile because "what" is not of object
```

It is possible to keep the original type and have a constraint to not allow a primitive with the keyword extends:

```
interface AnyKindOfObject {
  what: string;
}

interface ReusableInterface3<T extends object> {
  entity: T;
}

const d: ReusableInterface3<AnyKindOfObject> = { entity: a };
console.log(d.entity.what); // Compile
```

The `extends` keyword allows specifying the minimum structure that must be present in the object passed to the generic type. In that case, we were passing an object. However, we could extend any minimum structure, interface, or type:

```
interface ObjectWithId {
  id: number;
  what: string;
}

interface ReusableInterface4<T extends { id: number }> {
  entity: T;
}

const e: ReusableInterface4<AnyKindOfObject> = { entity: a }; // Doesn't compile
const f: ReusableInterface4<ObjectWithId> = { entity: { id: 1, what: "1" } }; // Compile
const g: ReusableInterface4<string> = { entity: "test" }; // Doesn't compile
```

The previous code example has two variables that do not compile. The first one, the variable is set to a wrong object. The third variable is set to a string, but the generic constraint cannot be fulfilled by the string because it doesn't have the id:number field. The second variable compiles because of the entity respect the constraint. Finally, here is an example of having a generic with a constraint that is an interface:

```
interface ReusableInterface5<T extends ObjectWithId> {
    entity: T;
}
```

Other than having access back to the full original type, generic with constraint allows accessing the constrain field from the class or function that implements the generic. The first code example, with `function`, has the constraint directly at the function signature. It allows accessing only the field from the constraint:

```
function funct1<T extends ObjectWithId>(p: T): void {
    console.log(`Access to ${p.what} and ${p.id}`);
}
```

Similarly, a class lets you use inside any of its functions, the field from the generic constraint. In the following code, the function loops the generic list of `T`. Since `T` is extending `ObjectWithId` that has `what` property and `id`; both are accessible:

```
class ReusableClass<T extends ObjectWithId>{
  public list: T[] = [];
  public funct1(): void {
```

```
    this.list.forEach((p) => {
      console.log(`Access to ${p.what} and ${p.id}`);
    });
  }
}
```

Generic and intersection

Generic and intersection work well together. It allows the use of an undetermined type and creates a second one with the combination of a known type or another generic. In the following code, there is a generic function that takes a type T that must respect to a minimum the structure of the User object. The return type of the function is the generic type passed by a parameter intersected by a new WithId structure. It means that whatever the type passed will be enhanced with the new structure. In the code, the Developer type is passed to the function and the function returns Developer+WithId. It is a new type, not defined anywhere, but is still strongly typed:

```
interface WithId {
  id: number;
}

interface User {
  name: string;
}

interface Developer extends User {
  favoriteLanguage: string;
}

function identifyUser<T extends User>(user: T): T & WithId {
  const newUser = (<any>Object).assign({}, user, { id: 1 });
  return newUser;
}

const user: Developer = { name: "Patrick", favoriteLanguage: "TypeScript"
};
const userWithId = identifyUser(user);
console.log(`${userWithId.name} (${userWithId.id}) favorite language
  is ${userWithId.favoriteLanguage}`);
```

The code shows that we can use the return type and have all three members available.

It is possible to intersect many generic types together, for example:

```
function merge<T, U>(obj1: T, obj2: U): T & U {
    return Object.assign({}, obj1, obj2);
}
```

The `merge` function takes two different types and merges them using the JavaScript `assign` function. The function returns the intersection of both types. If we dig into the definition of the `Object.assign` function, we realize that this one is also leveraging the intersection with generic. Here is the definition file of `Object.assign` for ES2015:

```
assign<T, U, V>(target: T, source1: U, source2: V): T & U & V;
```

Default generic

The more you work with generic, the more you may find that for a particular case in your system you are using always the same type. It could almost not be generic but be of a specific type. In that case, it is interesting to use a default type for your generic. A default generic type allows avoids having to specify a type. A default generic is also known as an optional type.

TypeScript uses the type specified in the generic signature after the equals sign:

```
interface BaseType<T = string> {
  id: T;
}
let entity1: BaseType;
let entity2: BaseType<string>;
let entity3: BaseType<number>;
```

Three variables are declared. The first and second ones are exactly the same: they expect an object with an `id` of a `string` type. The last is a number. The reason the first and second are exactly the same is that the first declaration relies on the default type. The default type is specified in the generic definition of the interface after the name of the type, `T`. The use of the equals signs allows the assignment.

In the case of multiple defaults, only optional typing can be used if no type is optional afterward. The following code shows the same interface, the first one does not compile because it has the optional generic type before a required type:

```
interface User<T = string, U> { // Does not compile
    id: T;
    name: U;
}
```

```
interface User<U, T = string> {
  id: T;
  name: U;
}
```

Default generic can have constraints and it deems to respect constraint with its default type. The following code does not work because the default type is set to be a number. However, the constraint mentions that the structure must have an id of type `number`:

```
interface WithId {
  id: number;
}

interface UserWithDefault<T extends WithId = number> { } // Does not compile
```

However, if we change the default type to be `User<number>` it compiles. The reason is that user interface has an `id` field of type `T`. The default type is not compatible with the constraint extended, which requires an `id` of a `number` type. This means that without explicitly mentioning the generic type of `User` in the default signature, the code does not compile:

```
interface User<T = string> {
  id: T;
}

interface WithId {
  id: number;
}

interface UserWithDefault<T extends WithId = User<number>> { }
// Does not compile because User<string>
interface UserWithDefault<T extends WithId = User { }
```

A default type is used when a type is not explicit or when TypeScript cannot infer the type.

Generic optional type

A generic type can be optional in a function or a class. When optional and generic, the type becomes an empty object or undefined:

```
function shows<T>(p1?: T): void {
  console.log(p1);
}
```

```
shows(); // p1 is {} | undefined
shows("123");
shows(123);
```

Providing a default value to an optional type changes the parameter from an empty object to the default type:

```
function shows<T = number>(p1?: T): void {
  console.log(p1);
}
shows(); // p1 is number | undefined
```

Generic constraints with a union type

There is some room for using a union in the `extends` clause of a generic definition. While you cannot use `discriminator`, you can compare against an array. The following object allows a type and an array of the same type. You can narrow down to any of the two types using `instanceOf` and manipulate the parameter value:

```
interface ObjectWithAge {
  kind: "ObjectWithAge";
  age: number;
}

function funct2<T extends ObjectWithAge | ObjectWithAge[]>(p: T): T {
  if (p instanceof Array) {
    return p[0];
  }
  return p;
}
```

Trying to extend two different objects with a discriminator does not work at the moment.

Restricting string choices with keyof

The use of string in JavaScript is omnipresent. One pattern is to access a member of an object dynamically with the square bracket:

```
interface Human {
  name: string;
  birthdate: Date;
  isHappy: boolean;
}
```

```
const me: Human = {
 name: "Patrick",
 birthdate: new Date(1912, 0, 1),
 isHappy: true
}

console.log(me["name"]);
```

The problem with the code is that `name` is a string and could be anything. We could set between brackets `firstname`, and the code would compile. At runtime, the console would show `undefined`. To avoid falling into the pitfall of selecting a member that does not exist, we can use `keyof`, which will return a union of all members of an object. The union is a `string literal` of all members' names.

Before going with `keyof`, create a `function` that tries to access a property by a string fail, without defining an index signature (see *Index signature* in this book):

```
function showMe1(obj: Human, field: string): void {
  console.log(obj[field]); // Does not compile
}
```

However, the same function with `keyof` will work without an index signature. The reason is that TypeScript knows that you do not try to access a field that might not exist. The goal of accessing with the square bracket is to access members that exist:

```
function showMe2(obj: Human, field: keyof Human): void {
  console.log(obj[field]);
}
```

The `keyof` allows specifying in a string format the only field from the type after the `keyof` keyword. In the code example before, only the string `name`, `birthdate` and `isHappy` can be entered without having the compiler show an error:

```
showMe2(me, "name"); // Compile
showMe2(me, "NOname"); // Does not compile
```

Limiting the access to members of a generic type

It is possible to use generic with `keyof` in a constraint to only specify in a string format member name from the generic object.

In the following code, we are passing an object in the first parameter, and in the second accepting only the member name of the first parameter object. The constraint syntax is the same using `extends` followed by `keyof` and the first generic type. The return type is the return type of the selected member, which is accessible by using the first generic with the index signature of the second generic:

```
function prop<TObject, TMember extends keyof TObject>(
  obj: TObject,
  key: TMember
): TObject[TMember] {
  return obj[key];
}

interface ObjectWithName {
  name: string;
  age: number;
}

const obj1: ObjectWithName = { name: "Patrick", age: 212 };
const result1: string = prop(obj1, "name");
const result2: number = prop(obj1, "age");
```

The syntax provides a good type safety, in terms of specifying members of an object that can be from a variety of potential types, and also provides safety in terms of the return type. If `name` changes from `string` to a rich object (with many members), the code consuming the return of this function will break at compilation time. It's the same if the name changes, the refactoring tool will change it. However, if the change is done without using any refactoring tool, the compiler will catch that the name is not a valid one.

The following code shows how `keyof` can be used to make sure a function returns the name of the desired member. The first time the function is called, it returns `name`; however, the second invocation does not compile because the name of the member does not exist in the generic type:

```
function nameof<T>(instance: T, key: keyof T): keyof T {
    return key;
}

const name1 = nameof(obj1, "name");
const name2 = nameof(obj1, "nasme"); // Does not compile
console.log(name1); // "name"
```

[123]

Reducing your type creation with mapped type

When you start typing all your objects, you may fall into the situation where you need to have almost the same type but with some minor differences. You may want the exact same property but all readable, when the main type has a few read-only types. You may want to have all field optionals to allow partial object updates or you may want to seal an object by making all its properties read-only. You might even want to have all your properties to be a string because your form handle string values only, but later has the real interface or type with the good type. TypeScript allows creating dynamic type from an existing one. This transformation of the type is named *mapped type*. Mapped type allows reducing the burden of duplicating an object just to change a property on the type, while keeping the same structure of your definition.

TypeScript comes with many mapped types that you can use without having to build your own mapped type. Here are two common ones:

```
type Readonly<T> = {
  readonly [P in keyof T]: T[P];
}

type Partial<T> = {
  [P in keyof T]?: T[P];
}
```

The first one, `Readonly`, takes a generic type and loops all its members and adds `readonly`. It also returns the same type with `T[P]`. The second one, `Partial`, adds the `?` character after the name, which means that every field becomes optional:

```
interface MyEntity {
  readonly id: number;
  name: string;
}

const e1: MyEntity = { id: 1, name: "Name1" };
```

If we want to have the variable to be sealed and completely not editable, we can use Readonly:

```
const e1: MyEntity = { id: 1, name: "Name1" };
const e2: Readonly<MyEntity> = e1;
e1.name = "I can change";
e2.name = "I cannot change"; // Does not compile
```

If you want to allow someone to modify only a part of your entity and then merge the result, you can use Partial:

```
function edit<T>(original: T, obj: Partial<T>): T {
  const returnObject: T = Object.assign({}, original, obj);
  return returnObject;
}

edit(e1, { name: "Super" }); // The returned object is: {id: 1, name: "Super"}
edit(e1, { memberNoExist: "Super" }); // Does not compile
```

You can create your own mapped type by using the type keyword and creating a name with an *in* operator to loop the member and defining the transformation. It is important to notice that we do not manipulate the data, only the type. It means that if you are changing the type that you still need to manipulate the object to have the expected shape that will fulfil the mapped type. Here are two examples of the custom type. The first one returns a string for all members. The second removes the Readonly. You can see the minus sign before the property, which indicates to TypeScript that the modifier of the member is taken away:

```
type Stringify<T> = { [P in keyof T]: string; };
type UnReadonly<T> = { -readonly [P in keyof T]: T[P]; };
```

Mapped type can be stacked to create a final type that combines all mapped types. In the following example, we stack two mapped types:

```
const e3: UnReadonly<Stringify<MyEntity>> = e1;
```

The code is legit but does not work. The reason is that TypeScript figures out that the e1.id is of type number and something tries to cast it into a string that does not occur automatically. As mentioned, a mapped type is only good as a cast and requires you to have the proper code.

Here is a quick and small function that does the trick. Do not use this code in production, since it does not cover the transformation into a string property (especially with `object` and `array`), but it illustrates the required transformation:

```
function castAllFieldToString<T>(obj: T): Stringify<T> {
  let returnValue: any = {};
  for (var property in obj) {
    if (obj.hasOwnProperty(property)) {
      returnValue[property] = obj[property].toString();
    }
  }
  return returnValue as Stringify<T>;
}

const e3: UnReadonly<Stringify<MyEntity>> = castAllFieldToString(e1);
e3.id = "123";
```

Generic type in TSX File

TSX is the equivalent of JSX, the JavaScript XML extension language. For a long period of time, TypeScript was supporting TSX but wasn't friendly with generic. The main reason is that TSX and the generic syntax share the angle brackets, which was causing the compiler to misinterpret the generic type when in a TSX file. However, the situation has changed, and TypeScript distinguishes when the square brackets are to explicitly define the type of a generic component. In the following snippet, you can see the `CallGenericComponent` that tries to render a generic component. The return is using an initial opening angle bracket to initialize the TSX component. The following and second opening angle bracket is to define the type:

```
interface MyTsxProps<T> {
  item: T;
}

class CallGenericComponent extends React.Component<{}>{
  public render(): JSX.Element {
    return <MyTsxComponent<string> item={"123"} />
  }
}

class MyTsxComponent<T> extends React.Component<MyTsxProps<T>>{
  // ...
}
```

The use of the angle brackets allows to avoids defining the component as a variable and having to instantiate it, which was not only required multiple lines but also to cast with any. Furthermore, the readability was compromised and the intention was unclear to an external pair of eyes.

Summary

In this chapter, we saw how to transform your code by using generic. TypeScript provides constraints to limit what can be passed into generic, and we saw how to leverage the constraint to guide the user as to what can be passed. We also saw how powerful the use of `keyof` is, allowing us to dynamically get members from a type. We saw how to manipulate type in a generic way, with mapped type.

7
Mastering the Art of Defining Types

In this chapter, we will see how to create types from libraries that we are not working directly with but importing inside our TypeScript project. The main difference is that when consuming code outside our project, we will not use TypeScript code directly, but its definition. The reason is that JavaScript is provided in those libraries, not TypeScript code. We will see how it is possible to master the art of creating definition files for code that does not provide them, allowing us to keep working in a strong environment.

This chapter covers the following:

- How to use a third-party library definition file
- How TypeScript can generate a definition file
- How to manually add a definition file for a JavaScript project
- How to merge types into an existing definition file
- How to create a definition file for a JavaScript project
- No need for a strong type but want to use a JavaScript library
- The need to use another module
- How to add a definition file to an extension of an existing module

How to use a third-party library definition file

TypeScript works well when it knows the type of every variable and function. However, when using third-party libraries written in JavaScript, you do not have a definition file. TypeScript is smart and tries to infer type as much as it can by leveraging the standard documentation JSDoc, but nothing beats a signature written with TypeScript rules. However, there are many useful libraries written in JavaScript that do not have TypeScript's types. A definition file fills the gap between JavaScript and TypeScript. For a third-party library, the idea is to use a definition file. The definition file source can come from a manual edition if the original library is written in JavaScript or generated automatically by TypeScript if coded in TypeScript.

To use a third-party library definition file, you need to have the file in our project. The TypeScript definition file is a .d.ts extension. TypeScript will search for a definition file in the `node_modules` folder as well as in our project. Because TypeScript uses the `node_modules`, it means it can fetch definition files from NPM. TypeScript has one of the most active GitHub repositories, which has over 4,200 definition files supported by the community. They are all accessible using NPM under `@types`. Here is an example of how to get JQuery definition files:

```
npm install @types/jquery --save-dev
```

The rising popularity of TypeScript made many libraries incorporate the definition file directly into their main npm package. For example, Redux, has `index.d.ts` at the root of the main `npm` package. It means that you may already have the definition files without noticing. The reason library brings the definition files directly in the NPM package is that the versions of the types are always synchronized with the code. It has also benefited people who use JavaScript and using a code editor that can read the definition file. Some code editors can leverage the definition file to provide autocomplete features.

Other than the `node_modules`, TypeScript reads the configuration `types` and `typeroots` in the `tsconfig.json` file. For further details, refer to Chapter 1, *Getting Started with TypeScript*.

If a definition file is missing for a third party, you can create one; create a type that sets to `any` the main export that would remove the type safety but be able to access anything. There is also the option to enhance an existing third-party library by merging new definitions into the existing one. We will cover this area in this chapter.

How typescript can generate a definition file

Even if the code is built in TypeScript, when it is time to share with the world, only the JavaScript files are published. The reason is to have everyone, including JavaScript and TypeScript developers, to use your code. It is better to publish TypeScript's types in a format where the sole purpose is to provide type capability instead of using a full TypeScript code. On the other hand, TypeScript can generate JavaScript files that allow a browser to interpret the code flawlessly. Having TypeScript generating two kinds of files, the definition file and the JavaScript file, open the compatibility for the developers and browsers. While the definition file can be crafted by hand, which is handy for a library written in JavaScript that wants to offer TypeScript support, it is faster and generates less errors to have it generated automatically. That being said, TypeScript is the best to produce automatically the definition, since it is present in the .ts file. This is why TypeScript has a compilation option to produce the definition at compilation time called `declaration`, which the path can be controlled by the other option `declarationDir`. Both options have been discussed in `Chapter 1`, *Getting Started with TypeScript*. Here is the line that allows the generation of the `definition` file from a TypeScript compilation:

```
"declaration": true
```

How to manually add a definition file for a JavaScript project

Many projects are written in JavaScript but still want to have TypeScript uses to the benefice of type. Or, some JavaScript projects produce TypeScript's definition files to have good support in their code editor. Finally, some people outside the main repository of the JavaScript library develop manual definition files for every TypeScript user to consume the library.

To create a definition file from a project that you do not own, you need to create a folder with the name of the module you want to add types to, and add an index.d.ts file. However, if you own the library, you can set the `types` or `typing` (they are synonyms) to the path and filename of the `definition` file. In the following code example, the definition file is set to `main.d.ts` under the `lib` folder. If the `types` or `typing` are not provided, the definition file must be called `index.d.ts` at the root of the package folder.

Mastering the Art of Defining Types

Using `index.d.ts` is the best practice because TypeScript is optimized to search for `index.d.ts` when doing module resolution, as well as having the file with the name of the module (followed by `.d.ts`):

```
{
"name": "your-library",
"main": "./lib/main.js",
"types": "./lib/main.d.ts"
}
```

As with `library`, all dependencies must be specified. This time, all the definition file libraries must be mentioned in the `package.json`. It is important to notice that we are not referring to the definition files in the `dev` dependencies, because we want to have all the types downloaded and installed by the consumer of our `definition` file library.

How to merge types into an existing definition file

Types can be written in several places and merged into a single set of definitions that TypeScript can rely on. The principle is that you may be able to extend existing definitions with your own. The merging capability is helpful when you have JavaScript code that can be enhanced with plugins or with extensions. For example, the library Redux has its definition files in its repository and NPM package. The library named `Redux-thunk` also has its definition file, which adds to Redux a new `dispatch` function signature that overrides the one defined by `redux`. The definition file relies on merging type to add its own definition of the dispatch into the `redux` module:

```
declare module "redux" {
   export interface Dispatch<S> {
   <R, E>(asyncAction: ThunkAction<R, S, E>): R;
 }
}
```

Merging type requires to have some knowledge of how TypeScript allows. The first rule is that all namespace can be defined more than once in one or many files. It means that you can define code inside many namespace scopes and that TypeScript will see it was all in the same namespace.

The content of a namespace is shared only if tagged as an exported element:

```
namespace Merge {
  export interface I1 { m1: string; }
}

namespace Merge {
  export interface I2 { m2: string; }
}
```

This can be written in a single namespace:

```
namespace Merge {
    export interface I1 { m1: string; }
    export interface I2 { m2: string; }
}
```

Similarly, interfaces can be merged:

```
interface Mergeable {
  m1: string;
}

interface Mergeable {
  m2: string;
}

const mergeInterface: Mergeable = { m1: "", m2: "" }
```

However, `type` does not act as an interface and does not allow to merge.

A class can have its definition enhanced by having an interface of the same name. So, it means that you can have the interface defined with the same name as the concrete class (in JavaScript) and be able to define a strongly typed definition. It also means that you can provide extension members of the class in the definition, if needed:

```
export interface Album { m1: string; m2: number; }
export class Album {
public m2: number = 12;
}
const a = new Album();
a.m1; // Not implemented but compile.
a.m2;
```

A namespace can be used to define a function variable. In JavaScript, it is possible to assign a variable to a function by using the function name and the dot notation. To define the type of this function, it requires specifying not only the parameter name and return type but also the variable. This is possible by defining a namespace with the function name:

```
function functionInJavaScript(param: string): string {
  return functionInJavaScript.variableOfFunction + param;
}
namespace functionInJavaScript {
  export let variableOfFunction = "";
}
```

It is possible to declare at the `global` scope an `interface` function:

```
declare global {
   interface Array<T> {
       toObservable(): Observable<T>;
   }
}
```

Creating a definition file for a JavaScript project

Today's world of open source reduces the barrier of examples. TypeScript has one of the most active repositories, which is the one that all the types of third-party libraries that do not have the definition file in their main repository. A quick look at a few libraries shows a fragmentation on how to write definition files. This is due to the high amount of different library structure. JavaScript has a global, modular, UMD, plugins, and global-modifying.

Definition file for global structure library

The epitome of a global library is JQuery with its popular dollar sign. Global library adds their functions and variables to the window scope. This can be done explicitly by using `window` or implicitly by defining a var. It does not use any import, export, or require functions.

To create a definition file for a global structure library, you can use many TypeScript keywords to define a type. In the case of a function, you can use `function` preceded by `declare` and write the signature of the function as you would do in an interface, without a body:

```
declare function myGlobalFunction(p1: string): string;
```

The keyword `declare` is there to say that the function is present somewhere else:

```
Let var1:string = myGlobalFunction("test");
```

If you have a type instead of a function declared at the global scope, you can use an interface. The keyword `declare` is omitted:

```
interface myGlobalType{
   name: string;
}
```

The global interface allows declaring a variable of a global type without prefixing the type by anything:

```
Let var1: myGlobalType={name:"test"};
```

A global interface allows specifying a type in a group of a cohesive element. It often represents a function scope:

```
declare namespace myScope{
  let var1: number;
  class MyClass{
  }
}

let x: number = myScope.var1;
let y: myScope.MyClass = new myScope.MyClass();
```

The namespace can include an interface to define an object, a type to define a variable of a specific type and to use a `function` for functions:

```
declare namespace myScope{
 interface MyObject{
    x: number;
 }

 type data = string;
 function myFunction():void{};
}
```

The usage of the object, variable, and function always uses the namespace name because it is exposed globally by the variable name:

```
let s: myScope.MyObject = { x: 5 };
let x: myScope.data = "test";
myScope.myFunction();
```

In this section, we saw how to define a global library that can have a global function or variable but also a global variable that can hold an object, a primitive of a function.

Definition file for module library

The `definition` file for a library is similar but also different. If you need to provide a definition file, it is recommended to name an `index.d.ts` with the following rules. First, there is an optional export declaration that is needed if the library supports UMD. This happens when the library exports a variable. The variable exposed in the following code example is `myScope`, where the whole module resides:

```
export as namespace myScope;
```

The next steps are to add every function directly to the definition file. There is no need to englobe the functions into a namespace. This is the same for an object:

```
export function myFunction(): void;
export interface MyObject{
 x: number;
}
export let data: string;
```

The usage of the function, interface, and variable would be like this in the actual code:

```
import {myFunction, MyObject, data} from "myScope";
myFunction();
x:MyObject = {x:1};
console.log(data);
```

The remaining feature would be to have an object inside your module:

```
export namespace myProperty{
    export function myFunction2(): void;
}
```

Chapter 7

Here is the actual usage of the namespace, which, like the functions, object, and data, is available in two formats. The first is with the explicit callout of the element to be retrieved from the module or the second with the star, which gets the whole content definition into the alias:

```
Import {myProperty} from "myScope";
myProperty.myFunction2();
//or
Import * from my from "myScope"
my.myProperty.myFunction2();
```

However, in some cases, this won't work. It depends how the JavaScript module is written. The following code works for modern module creation. It uses the declare statement with a module. The module name must be the library name between quotes. Inside the module, you can define your export for `CommonJs/Amd` with `export =`, followed by what you want to export by default. In the following code, the class `MessageFormat` is the default export. It is possible to not have a `CommonJs/Amd` export and to export every type. You can export a namespace that contains many types as well:

```
declare module "modulenamehere" {
  type Msg = (params: {}) => string;
  type SrcMessage = string | SrcObject;
  interface SrcObject {
  m1: SrcMessage;
}

class MessageFormat {
  constructor(message: string);
  constructor();
  compile: (messages: SrcMessage, locale?: string) => Msg;
}

export = MessageFormat ; // CommonJs/AMD export syntax
}

// Usage:

import MessageFormat from "modulenamehere";
const mf = new MessageFormat("en");
const thing = mf.compile("blarb");
```

JavaScript library without a definition file

If you need to use a third-party library that does not have any definition file, you can start by a single-line declaration. You need to create a file with the name of the module with the extension `.d.ts` and add this single line:

```
declare module "*";
```

This won't give you any Intellisence, auto-completion, but the file will be importable inside your TypeScript file without any issue with the compiler. You can start with this one-line approach and then slowly move to a more elaborate definition.

Using another module from a definition file

You may need to consume another module from your definition file. The reason might be to get types from another library. To be able to use the type of another library, you can use `import *` and assign an alias with `as` from the type you want to refer in your `definition` file:

```
declare module "react-summernote" {
  import * as React from "react";
  let ReactSummernote: React.ComponentClass<any>;
  export default ReactSummernote;
}
```

Adding a definition file to an extension of an existing module

The idea is to use the `declare` and the name of the module to extend. A system can have more than one declaration of the same module, allowing the possibility to add an exported `type`, `function`, `interface`, or `class`. The following code shows also the usage of another module that is used by the extension of the module:

```
import * as extendMe from "moduleToExtend";
import * as other from "anotherModule";

declare module "moduleToExtend" {
export function theNewMethod(x: extendMe.aTypeInsideModuleToExtend):
other.anotherTypeFromAnotherModule;
export interface ExistingInterfaceFromModuleToExtend {
```

```
    newMember: string;
}

export interface NewTypeForModuleToExtend {
    size: number;
}
}
```

Summary

In this chapter, we illustrated how to work with definition files. We explained many facets of how to work with definition files as well as many details to facilitate the creation of definition, depending on how the JavaScript code was written.

In this book, we summarized everything that is essential to get started with TypeScript. This quick starting guide goal was to set the table for a wonderful meal that you can prepare with TypeScript. The book talked about how to code from a basic concept with primitive type to a more advanced one with generic. Hopefully, you will be as delighted as I am working with a typed language that is close to JavaScript but more powerful in terms of maintainability, as well as being easier to read. Thanks to type and TypeScript, web development is safer, more productive, and enjoyable.

Other Books You May Enjoy

If you enjoyed this book, you may be interested in these other books by Packt:

TypeScript 2.x By Example
Sachin Ohri

ISBN: 978-1-78728-003-8

- Design your first project in Visual Studio
- Learn about the different data types in TypeScript
- Create web applications in an object-oriented fashion using TypeScript
- Build a Trello application using TypeScript's complex features.
- Explore the tools available in a web application ecosystem to write unit test cases
- Deploy web applications to cloud and assign resources to the application

TypeScript Microservices
Parth Ghiya

ISBN: 978-1-78883-075-1

- Get acquainted with the fundamentals behind microservices.
- Explore the behavioral changes needed for moving from monolithic to microservices.
- Dive into reactive programming, Typescript and Node.js to learn its fundamentals in microservices.
- Understand and design a service gateway and service registry for your microservices.
- Maintain the state of microservice and handle dependencies.
- Perfect your microservice with unit testing and Integration testing.
- Develop a microservice, secure it, deploy it, and then scale it

Leave a review - let other readers know what you think

Please share your thoughts on this book with others by leaving a review on the site that you bought it from. If you purchased the book from Amazon, please leave us an honest review on this book's Amazon page. This is vital so that other potential readers can see and use your unbiased opinion to make purchasing decisions, we can understand what our customers think about our products, and our authors can see your feedback on the title that they have worked with Packt to create. It will only take a few minutes of your time, but is valuable to other potential customers, our authors, and Packt. Thank you!

Index

A
abstraction 88, 90
any
  using 62
array
  destructuring 70

B
baseUrl 16
boolean type 34

C
cast
  versus explicit type 64
casting 104
class
  about 78
  comparing 108, 110
  field definition, reducing with value set at construction time 81
  instantiation 78, 80
  private, using for encapsulation 80
  protected, using for encapsulation 80
  public, using for encapsulation 80
command-line interface (CLI) 7
configuration file 20
const
  about 27
  declaring 31
constructed object
  creating 64
constructor
  enforcing, from interface 92

D
declaration 19
declare
  versus const 74
  versus let 74
  versus var 74
default generic 119
definition file
  adding, to existing module 138
  avoiding, for JavaScript library 138
  creating, for JavaScript project 134
  generating, with typescript 131
  manually adding, for JavaScript project 131
  module, using 138
  types, merging 132
  using, for global structure library 134
  using, for module library 136
discriminator
  about 100
  using, for type identification 100, 102

E
ECMAScript
  about 22
  lib 23
  target 23
explicit type
  versus cast 64

F
function expression 50
function statement 50
functions 48

G

generic code
  reusability 113
generic optional type 120
generic type
  constaining 116
  data structure 115
  in TSX File 126
  member access, limiting 123
  working, with intersection 118
Grunt 8, 10
Gulp 10, 12

I

implicit type 51, 52
index signature
  dictionary type, setting 56
  set type, setting 56
  versus map 60
inheritance
  type, merging 69
instanceof
  limitations 98
interface
  constructor, enforcing 92
  intersecting 68
  using, in object-oriented 87, 88
  versus type 69
intersect
  type, combining 66
intersection
  working, with generic 118

K

keyof
  string choices, restricting 121

L

let
  about 27
  declaring 29, 30
literal type guard 102

M

map
  about 59
  versus index signature 60
mapped type
  type creation, reducing 124
mapRoot 17
module 22
moduleResolution 22

N

NodeJS
  URL 7
non-primitive group
  about 38
  any type, avoiding 40
  conscribed set, defining of constants with enum 43
  never type, using 40
  string literals, versus string 46
  type, enforcing in list 42
  unknown type 42
  void 39
non-public constructor
  use cases 83
NPM/CLI 14
null type
  about 35
  versus undefined type 97
numeric separators 33

O

object literal
  about 63
  versus, object using from class 84, 87
Object
  using 62
object
  using 62
  versus Object 61
open-ended 69
optional type
  intersecting 68

R

readonly keyword
  using 91

S

sourceMap 17
sourceRoot 17
static member 82, 83
string 33
string interpolation 34
Symbol 37

T

tagged union 102
third-party library definition file
  using 130
tuple 72, 74
type assertion 106, 108
type casting
  benefits 104, 106
type
  combining, with intersect 66
  destructuring 70
  merging, with inheritance 69
typed function
  crafting 48, 50
typeof
  used, for comparing at runtime 96
  used, for comparing with design time 96
TypeScript compiler (tsc)
  about 14, 15
  baseUrl 16
  configuration file 20
  declaration 19
  ECMAScript 22
  exclude 18
  files 18
  files location 16
  include 18
  mapRoot 17
  module 21
  ModuleResolution 21
  outDir 16
  outfile 18
  paths 16
  restrictions 23
  rootDir 16
  sourceMap 17
  sourceRoot 17
  StricNullChecks 24
  strict 24
  StrictFunctionTypes 24
  StrictPropertyInitialization 24
  type 19
  typeRoots 19
  types 19
TypeScript
  number 32
  primitives, enhancing 31

U

undefined type
  about 36
  versus null type 97
union
  element type, obtaining 97
  generic constraints 121
user-defined guard pattern 102, 104

V

var
  about 27
  declaring 28
variables
  with many types 65

W

Webpack 12, 14

Printed in Great Britain
by Amazon